NEW EDITION

LADO ENGLISH SERIES

BOOK **2**

by **Robert Lado**

Professor of Linguistics
School of Languages and Linguistics
Georgetown University·

in collaboration with

Jerome C. Ford
Bernadette Sheridan, I.H.M.
Annette Silverio-Borges

Regents Publishing Company, Inc.

Illustrations by Bill Kresse

Table of Contents

Preface   i

Unit 1   **Talking about work**   1
Information questions with *do*   3
Numbers 21 to 109   7
My name is David Horgan 11
Sound [š] : *shin* 13

Unit 2   **Talking about lunch** 14
Information questions with *when* 17
Time expressions 20
Parts of the day 24
Months of the year 25
In North America there are four seasons 28
Contrast [č] *chin* and [š] *shin* 31

Unit 3   **Going to the dentist's office** 32
The future with *going to* 34
The negative with *going to* 36
Yes/no questions with *going to* 39
Short answers to yes/no questions with *going to* 41
Nancy and Peter McCall like sports 45
Contrast [f] *fan* and [v] *van* 47

Unit 4   **Taking a business trip** 48
Information questions with *going to* 50
Short answers to information questions 53
Ben and Ruth Miller live in Chicago 57
Sound [b] : *band* 59

Unit 5   **Going to a convention** 60
The past of *be* 62
The negative of *was* and *were* 65
Yes/no questions with the past of *be* 67
Short answers with the past of *be* 70
Information questions with the past of *be* 73

Every summer Catherine has a two-week
vacation 76
Contrast [b] *band* and [v] *van* 79

Unit 6   **Discussing a television program** 80
The regular past 82
Yes/no questions in the past 86
Catherine Wells was at home on Monday night 91
Sound [e] : *net* 93

Unit 7   **Discussing the football game** 94
The irregular past 96
Negative statements in the past 100
Short answers with *did* and *didn't* 102
Steve and Michael at the museum 106
Sound [ə] : *nut* 108

Unit 8   **Discussing a recent event** 109
Information questions in the past 112
Information questions about the verb phrase 115
in, on 118
Absent-minded Mr. Newton 122
Contrast [e] *net* and [ə] *nut* 124

Unit 9   **Seeing a friend unexpectedly** 125
Past progressive form 127
Negative past progressive form 130
Yes/no questions in the past progressive 132
Short answers to yes/no questions in the past
progressive 134
Information questions with the past progressive 136
John read a science magazine yesterday 141
Sound [θ] : *ether* 143

Unit 10   **Arriving late for work** 144
General questions with *happen* 146
Subject questions 151
Dear Olga, Christmas is coming soon 155
Contrast [s] *sink* and [θ] *think* 157

Key to pronunciation symbols 158

Vocabulary list 160

Index 167

Preface

The second edition of the *Lado English Series* is a complete course in English consisting of six carefully graded levels, with a textbook, workbook, teacher's manual, and cassettes for each level. The central objective of the series is to help students in the complex business of learning to understand, speak, read, and write English. In the new edition, careful attention has been given to the importance of learning to use these four skills for meaningful communication.

The chief innovative feature of the second edition is "contextualization," that is, the placing of all new structures and vocabulary in meaningful contexts, so that the student is always sure of the meaning of the sentences being presented or practiced. New "conversations" are introduced with a background situation which places them in a natural communicative setting. The substitution drills which formerly followed the conversation section have been transformed into "adaptations," which relate structures introduced in the dialogue to other situations in which they may be used. The "practices" are often centered on a context, and are usually accompanied by pictures, which clarify the meaning of each sentence, and provide the student with non-verbal cues. In general, the exercises in the new edition are designed to guide the student to a more creative use of the language in activities that closely approximate a normal communicative situation. All this has been achieved while maintaining the advantages of graded, organized learning.

The second edition has retained the same qualities of simplicity of presentation and transparent organization evident in the previous edition. Each unit of the student's text is divided into sections with clear, single-word headings indicating the purpose of the sections: *Conversation, Adaptation, Study, Practice, Speak, Read, Think,* and *Pronounce.*

Each Conversation in the first three books is short, for easier dramatization. It introduces practical topics and useful sentences, and provides a context for the presentation of new material in the unit. A background situation, which can be found in the teacher's manual, describes an appropriate context for the conversation. Intonation lines show the most usual intonation for each sentence, although many other intonations are also possible. These lines represent the four intonation levels of English: low, mid, high, and extra high. The sharp corners used in the previous edition have been replaced with curves, which more accurately represent a change from one level to another. A dot on an intonation line indicates the principal stress in each sentence.

The Adaptation section following each conversation takes up significant parts of the dialogue, usually a question and answer or a statement and comment. The student modifies these sentence pairs with the help of vocabulary cues, thus creating short dialogues which adapt the structures of the conversation to new situations.

The Study sections present grammatical points in simple, easy-to-read frames which help the student visualize each point quickly. A great effort has been made to find the clearest method of presentation for each structure. At the bottom of each frame are recommendations or rules for the use of the grammar point involved.

A Practice section follows each study frame. It consists of exercises which give the student a chance to practice in context the structures just presented. Experience has shown that students master the grammar most quickly when they understand it and use it at the same time. "Contextualization" has resulted in a major reworking of the Practice section. The exercises are made up of sentences which make contextual sense in addition to exemplifying the rule or feature of the study frame. In many cases an entire exercise relates to a single context. In others, responses depend on information supplied by pictures.

The Speak section focuses on using newly learned vocabulary and grammar in a variety of situations. The dialogues in this section are not to be memorized, but are rather to be read aloud and acted out by pairs or groups of students. The dialogues are then gradually modified until students are using the basic outline they provide to express real information about themselves.

The Read section combines the material presented in the unit with material from previous units in interesting reading passages which are to be read silently for meaning. Some new vocabulary is generally included as well. Through the use of these passages, the student's reading skill is developed gradually, moving from a supporting position in Book 1 to a position of major importance in Books 4, 5, and 6.

A Think section appears in every unit beginning with Book 2. It provides an opportunity for the student to use English more freely, and focuses on thought as the natural stimulus for the use of language. The pictures in this section are meant to encourage students to use new structures and vocabulary more creatively, the creative use of language being an essential part of the process of attaining competence in another language.

The Pronounce sections focus on elements of pronunciation which may cause problems both in understanding spoken English and in speaking it. These sections progressively treat all the phonemes of English. Facial diagrams provide a graphic description of the articulation of each sound. These sections also deal with consonant clusters, and particular pronunciation problems due to English spelling, stress, and intonation.

Every workbook after Workbook 1 begins with a Refresher Unit covering the material taught in the preceding level. It consists of a diagnostic test which singles out the points of pronunciation and grammar the students have not yet mastered, a review section which enables the student to selectively review these points, and a second diagnostic test to check whether all the material has been learned. This new unit will provide a useful review not only for those students who have completed the previous course, but also for those who have completed different curricula.

The six Workbooks are designed to complement the learning activities covered in the textbooks. They offer additional exercises to help students master the material in each unit, with the focus on listening, reading, and writing. They also provide conversational activities which can be done in groups.

The Teacher's Manuals have been thoroughly revised and expanded. There is now a separate manual for each textbook. Each page of the manual includes a reduced copy of the corresponding page from the textbook for easy reference. The answers to all the exercises are given together with the reduced page. All the new vocabulary presented in the unit is listed at the beginning of each section. This is followed by a detailed explanation of how to teach the section. Many suggestions for games are also given, so that students can have the chance to practice English in less formal situations. Answers to all workbook exercises can be found in the appendix.

There is a set of Cassettes for each textbook. They give the students the opportunity to listen to native speech, and can be used outside of class to provide extra speaking and listening practice.

It is our hope that the second edition will be even more useful and effective than the first, and we are sure that you will find this edition both appealing and highly functional for the task of teaching your students to communicate in English.

ROBERT LADO
Washington, D.C.

Unit 1

Conversation:
Talking about work

Steve: Where do you work?
Sally: I work in a department store.
Steve: What do you do?
Sally: I sell radios.
Steve: How do you go to work?
Sally: I go by bus. It's fast.

Where do you work?

I work in a department store.

What do you do?

I sell radios.

How do you go to work?

I go by bus. It's fast.

Adaptation

Construct two-line dialogues like the model. Use the cues.

1. work?
   in a department store.

   Where do you work?
   I work in a department store.

   study?
   at the library.

   Where do you study _____?
   I study at the library _____.

   eat?
   in the kitchen.

   Where do you eat _____?
   I eat, in the kitchen _____.

   live?
   in Cleveland.

   Where do you Live _____?
   I Live in Cleveland _____.

2. do?
   sell radios.

   What do you do?
   I sell radios.

   do?
   drive a bus.

   What do you do? _____?
   I drive a bus _____.

   make?
   shoes.

   What do you make _____?
   I make shoes _____.

   read?
   history books.

   What do you read _____?
   I read history books _____.

3. go to work?
   bus.

   How do you go to work?
   I go by bus.

   go to school?
   subway.

   How do you go to school _____?
   I go by subway _____.

   go home?
   car.

   How do you go home _____?
   I go by car _____.

   go to St. Louis?
   plane.

   How do you go to St Luis _____?
   I go by plane _____.

2

Information questions in the present tense: *Where do you work?*

Notice the position of the question words **where, what, how,** and **who(m):**

Do you live	**on Walnut Street?**	No.
Where do you live?		On Oak Street.
Does Sally sell	**shoes?**	No.
What does Sally sell?		Radios.
Do they sing	**badly?**	No.
How do they sing?		Well.
Do you work with	**Bill?**	No.
Who(m) do you work with?		Sarah.

Where ▶ places: on Oak Street, in Boston

What ▶ things: shoes, radios

How ▶ manner: well, badly, fast, slowly, by bus

Who(m) ▶ people: Bill, Sarah

Place the appropriate question word at the beginning of the question.

Who is used in conversation. **Whom** is used in formal writing, but never in subject questions.

3

Practice

1. Answer the questions according to the pictures.

Where does Sally work, in a factory
or in a department store?
▶ *She works in a department store.*

What does she sell, clocks
or radios?
▶ *She sells radios.*

Where does she eat lunch,
at home or at work?
▶ She eats lunch at work

Who does she eat with,
John or Steve?
▶ She eats with john.

What do Sally and John like,
soup or sandwiches?
▶ they like sandwiches.

What do they drink,
milk or soda?

▶ they drink milk.

Where does John live, on Smith
Avenue or on Hill Street?

▶ He Lives Hill street.

How does he go to work,
by bus or by car?

▶ He goes to work by bus.

Who does he go to work with,
Charles or Sally?

▶ He goes to work with
charles.

Charles

2. Ask questions with **where, who, how,** or **what.** Then answer the
   questions according to the pictures.

Does Steve feel fine?
No, he doesn't.
How does he feel?
He feels sick.

5

Do Steve and Sally live in New York?
No, they don't.
Where do they live?
They live in Philadelphia.

Philadelphia

Does Steve work with Sally?
No, he doesn't.
Who does he work ?
He works with Michael .

Michael

Does Michael drive a bus?
No, he doesn't.
What does he drive ?
He drives a car .

Does Michael drive slowly?
No, he doesn't.
How does drive ?
He drives fast .

Do you go to work by plane?
No, I don't.
How do you go to work ?
I go to work by bus .

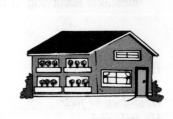

Do you eat dinner in a restaurant?
No, I don't.
Where do you eat ?
I eat dinner at home .

Do you eat dinner with your friends?
No, I don't.

How do you eat dinner ?
I eat dinner with my family .

my family

Do you sleep badly?
No, I don't.

How do you sleep ?
I sleep well .

opposite
Z-Z-Z-Zz

Do you sleep in the kitchen?
No, I don't.

Where do you sleep. ?
I Sleep in my bedroom .

Study 2

Numbers 21-109: *There are fifty-two weeks in a year.*

Notice the formation of the numbers 21-109:

20 twenty	1 one	21 twenty-one 31 thirty-one
30 thirty	2 two	22 twenty-two 32 thirty-two
40 forty	3 three	23 twenty-three 33 thirty-three
50 fifty	4 four	24 twenty-four 34 thirty-four
60 sixty	**+** 5 five	25 twenty-five 35 thirty-five
70 seventy	6 six	26 twenty-six 36 thirty-six
80 eighty	7 seven	27 twenty-seven 37 thirty-seven
90 ninety	8 eight	28 twenty-eight 38 thirty-eight
100 one hundred	9 nine	29 twenty-nine 39 thirty-nine

Combine the tens with the units:

> twenty + one ▶ twenty-one
> twenty + two ▶ twenty-two

Use a hyphen (-) between the tens and the units (but not between **one** and **hundred, two** and **hundred,** etc.):

> 21, 22 twenty-one, twenty-two, . . .
> 101, 102 one hundred one, one hundred two, . . .

Stress the unit in speaking:

> twenty-óne, twenty-twó, . . .

Practice

1. Read these numbers.

    24, 36, 49, 52, 60, 75, 88, 91, 100, 101

2. Read these sentences.

    I want 6 apples.
    Please give me 18 eggs.
    12 is a dozen.

    A dollar is 100 cents.
    A quarter is 25 cents.

    There are 30 days in November.
    February has only 28 days.
    There are 7 days in a week.
    There are 52 weeks in a year.
    There are 24 hours in a day.
    An hour is 60 minutes.
    A minute is 60 seconds.

3. Addresses: Say the numbers in groups of two. Divide from the end.

2468 ▶   24 68 ▶   twenty-four sixty-eight
214 ▶   2 14 ▶   two fourteen
320 ▶   3 20 ▶   three twenty
308 ▶   3 08 ▶   three o eight

4. Read these addresses.

I live at 2468 Kennedy Street.
John lives at 6692 Hill Street.
Helen lives at 214 New York Avenue.
What's Paul's address? It's 853 Coleman Street.
Vincent lives at 2238 Boston Avenue.
His cousin lives at 209 Johnson Street.

5. Answer these questions individually.

Where do you live?
Where does your cousin live?
Where do your friends live?
What's your telephone number?
What's your friend's telephone number?

Speak

1.   **Joseph:** Where do you buy your shirts?
      David: I buy them in a department store.
      Joseph: How do you like them?
      David: They're nice.

2. **Janet:** Where do you work?
   Jean: I work in the new cafeteria.
   Janet: Do you know Mr. Smith?
   Jean: No, I don't.
   Janet: Who do you know there?
   Jean: I only know Mrs. Weber. She's the manager.

3. **Steve:** Where's Sally?
   Michael: She's at home. She's sick.
   Steve: Where does she live?
   Michael: She lives on Main Street.
   Steve: Do you know her address?
   Michael: Yes. It's 1624 Main Street.

My name is David Horgan. I live with my family at 257 Kennedy Street. We live in an apartment. There are five rooms in our apartment: three bedrooms, a kitchen, and a living room. I have one brother and two sisters. My father is a salesman. He sells cars. My mother is a bookkeeper. She works in a drugstore. My brother and my sisters and I are students. My brother is in elementary school. My sisters go to high school and I go to City College. I study English, psychology, history, and chemistry. I study very hard. In the evening, I work in a garage. I make forty-five dollars a week.

11

Answer these questions.

1. What is the boy's name?
2. Who does he live with?
3. Where does he live?
4. What does his father do?
5. Where does his mother work?
6. Who goes to high school?
7. Where does David study?
8. What does he study?
9. How does he study?
10. Where does he work?
11. What is his salary?

Think

These people are Sally's friends. Tell something about each person.

John

Steve

Laura

Jean

David

Janet

Pronounce

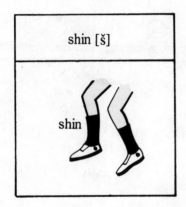

shin [š]

shin

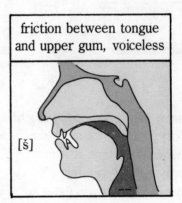

friction between tongue and upper gum, voiceless

[š]

shin	she	Chicago
ship	short	sharp
English	Spanish	Patricia

Is Patricia English?
No. She's Spanish.

Is she in Washington?
No. She's in Chicago.

Is she tall or short?
She's short.

13

Unit 2

Conversation:
Talking about lunch

Laura: When do you eat lunch?
Sally: I eat lunch at twelve o'clock.
Laura: What time is it now?
Sally: It's eleven thirty.
Laura: Who do you eat with?
Sally: I usually eat with John.

When do you eat lunch?

I eat lunch at twelve o'clock.

What time is it now?

It's eleven thirty.

Who do you eat with?

I usually eat with John.

Adaptation

Construct two-line dialogues like the model. Use the cues.

1. eat lunch?
   at twelve o'clock.

When do you eat lunch?
I eat lunch at twelve o'clock.

have dinner?
at seven o'clock.

When do you have dinner?
I have dinner at seven o'clock

do the dishes?
at eight thirty.

When do you do the dishes ?
I do the dishes at .
eight thirty

go to bed?
at midnight.

When do you go to bed ?
I got to bed at midnight

2. eleven thirty.

What time is it now?
It's eleven thirty.

twelve o'clock.

What time is it now ?
It's twelve o'clock .

15

nine o'clock

What time is it now?
It's nine o'clock.

noon

What time is it now?
It's noon o'clock.

3. eat with?
   John.

Who do you eat with?
I usually eat with John.

talk to?
Bob and Beth.

who do you talk to?
I usually talk with Bob and Beth.

work with?
Mrs. Murphy.

who do you work with?
I usually work with Mrs. Murphy.

play tennis with?
Barbara.

Who do you play tennis with?
I usually play tennis with Barbara.

Study 1

Information questions with **when:** *When do you eat lunch?*

Notice the use of **when:**

Do you get up at seven o'clock? No.

When do you get up?

Do you make your bed in the morning? No.

When do you make your bed?

Do you wash your face before breakfast? No.

When do you wash your face?

Use **when** for time information.

Practice

1. Use the cues to make short dialogues like the model.

get up at seven o'clock?

At six o'clock.

Do you get up at seven o'clock?
No, I don't.
When do you get up?
At six o'clock.

eat lunch at twelve o'clock?

At one o'clock.

_____?
No, I don't _____.
When do you eat _____?
at one o'clock _____. 17

wash your hands
after lunch?

_____ ?
_____ .
_____ ?

Before lunch.

_____ .

read the newspaper
in the afternoon?

_____ ?
No I don't _____ .
when do you _____ ?

In the morning.

_____ .

go home at five
o'clock?

_____ ?
_____ .
_____ ?

At 4:30.

_____ .

listen to music in
the morning?

_____ ?
_____ .
_____ ?

At night.

_____ .

2. Answer these questions according to the picture.

Where does Sally eat lunch,
at home or at work?
▶ *She eats lunch at work.*

When does she eat lunch,
at twelve or at one?

▶ She eats Lunch a twelve.

Who does she talk to, Laura
Bond or Jane Ross?

▶ She talks to Laura Bond.

Laura Bond

Where do they work, in a
school or in a hospital?

▶ they work in a hospital

What do I drink, water or
milk?

▶ You drink water

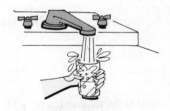

How do they go to work, by
car or by taxi?

▶ They go to work by car

3. Answer these questions about yourself. Answer them individually.

What do you study, English or Chinese?
▶ *I study English.*

How do you feel, well or sick?
▶ I feel Well

19

When do you make your bed, in the morning or the evening?

▶ I make my bed in the morning.

When do you wash your face, before breakfast or after breakfast?

▶ I wash my face before breakfast

How do you eat lunch, fast or slowly?

▶ I eat lunch slowly.

Who do you eat dinner with, your family or your friends?

▶ I eat dinner with my family.

Where do you watch television, in class or at home?

▶ I watch t.v at home

Study 2

Time expressions: *What time is it? It's two o'clock.*

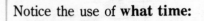

Notice the use of **what time:**

Is it **one o'clock?** No.

What time is it?

Use **what time** for clock time.

Notice the possible answers:

What time is it?

It's three o'clock.

It's five (minutes) after one.

It's twelve o'clock.

It's noon.

It's midnight.

It's a quarter after four.

It's twenty-five (minutes) to two.

It's half past four.
It's four thirty.

It's a quarter to three.

It's ten (minutes) to seven.

For official or exact time, use this form:

It's 6:10.   (It's six ten.)
It's 7:28.   (It's seven twenty-eight.)
It's 7:55.   (It's seven fifty-five.)
It's 8:05.   (It's eight o five.)

Use **o'clock** only on the hour: **It's two o'clock,
It's three o'clock,** etc.

Use **after** until half past the hour:
It's ten after six.
Use **to** from half past the hour
until just before the hour:
It's twenty to seven.

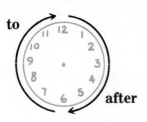

Practice

This is Laura Bond's schedule every day. What time does she do these
things?

Laura gets up at

▶ *Laura gets up
at seven o'clock.*

She eats breakfast at
▶ quarter to eight

She goes to work at
▶ ten after eight

She has coffee at
▶ ten thirty

She eats lunch at
▶ twelve thirty

She reads the newspaper at
▶ a quarter after twelve

She goes home at
▶ five o'clock

She takes a walk at
▶ five thirty

She eats dinner at
▶ ten to seven

She goes to bed at
▶ eleven o'clock

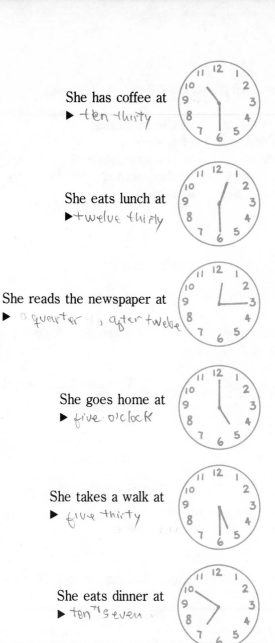

Study 3

Parts of the day: *We go to school in the morning.*

We eat breakfast	**in the morning.**
We eat lunch	**at noon.**
We study	**in the afternoon.**
We eat dinner	**in the evening.**
We sleep	**at night.**

Practice

1. Answer the questions with parts of the day.

When do we study?
▶ *We study in the evening.*

When does Sally eat lunch?
▶ She eats lunch ats noon.

When do we sleep?
▶ we sleep at night

When do Laura and Harold Bond eat dinner?
▶ they eat in the evening dinner

When do we get up?
▶ we get up in the morning

When do they eat breakfast?
▶ they eat breakfast in the morning.

When does Sally go to work?
▶ She goes to work in the morning

When do they go to bed?
▶ they go to bed at night.

2. Answer the questions individually with clock time and parts of the day.

When do you get up?
▶ *I get up at 7:15 in the morning.*

When do you eat breakfast?
▶

When do you eat dinner?
▶ *I eat dinner at 7:30 in the evening.*

When do you go to work?
▶

When do you get up?
▶

When do you study?
▶

When do you eat lunch?
▶

When do you go to bed?
▶

When do you eat dinner?
▶

When do you go to sleep?
▶

When do you do the dishes?
▶

Study 4

Months of the year: *January, February* . . .

Learn the twelve months of the year:

January	April	July	October
February	May	August	November
March	June	September	December

Learn the poem about the months of the year:

Thirty days have September,
April, June, and November;
February has twenty-eight.
All the rest have thirty-one,
Except in leap year
When February has twenty-nine.

Learn the hand method for remembering the number of days in each month:

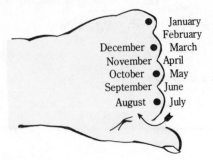

December ● March
November ⟨ April
October ● May
September ⟨ June
August ● ⟩ July

January
February

The months that coincide with the knuckles (●) have thirty-one days.

1. Say the months of the year.
2. Say the poem: "Thirty days have September, . . ."
3. Answer these questions.
   What months have 30 days?
   What months have 31 days?
   What month has 28 days?
   When does February have 29 days?

1. **Mr. Bond:** What time is the last train to Washington?
   Mr. Gómez: It's at ten o'clock.
   Mr. Bond: What time is it now?
   Mr. Gómez: It's five minutes after ten.

26

2. **Steve:** When is the last train to New York City?
   Clerk: It's at two o'clock.
   Steve: Is it at two o'clock in the afternoon?
   Clerk: No. It's at two o'clock in the morning.

3. **Sally:** Where are you from?
    Jean: I'm from Minnesota.
   Sally: How is the weather there?
    Jean: It's hot in the summer and cold in the winter.
   Sally: Do you go ice-skating in the winter?
    Jean: Yes, I do. The ice is good from December to March.

Read

Spring   Summer

In North America there are four seasons: spring, summer, fall, and winter. Each season is three months. The months of spring are March, April, and May. Officially, spring begins on March 21st.* It is usually cold and windy in March, but there are some warm days. In April it rains, but May is beautiful. The plants and trees become green, and there are flowers of many colors.

Summer begins on June 22nd.** The summer months are June, July, and August. It is very hot in the summer. School ends and vacation begins. People go on picnics and go to the beach. Summer is always too short.

Answer the questions.

1. What are the four seasons in North America?
2. When does spring begin?
3. How is the weather in March?
4. When does it rain?
5. When do the plants and trees become green?
6. How is the weather in the summer?
7. What do people do in the summer?

* 21st=twenty-first
** 22nd=twenty-second

Fall

Winter

After summer comes fall. It begins on September 23rd.* The fall months are September, October, and November. The weather is nice in September, but school begins and vacation ends. In October the leaves change color. They become yellow, red, and brown. The colors are very beautiful. But then the leaves fall from the trees.

Winter is the cold season. It begins on December 22nd.** The winter months are December, January, and February. It is usually cold in December, but people are very happy at Christmas. In many places it snows in the winter. Children play in the snow, and people go skiing and ice-skating.

Answer the questions.

1. When does school begin?
2. When do the leaves change color?
3. When does it snow?
4. What do people do in the winter?
5. Is January a cold month in your country?
6. What are the seasons in your country?
7. How is the weather in each season in your country?

* 23rd=twenty-third
** 22nd=twenty-second

Think

How is the weather in these months in Nebraska?

January

March

May

August

November

December

Contrast [č] and [š].

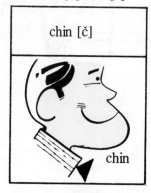

chin [č]

chin

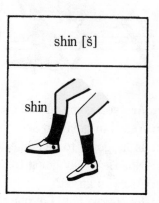

shin [š]

shin

chin	French	shin	Spanish
children	teacher	she	English
Charles	each	ship	Patricia
Chile	chocolate	Chicago	sugar

Is the teacher Spanish?
No. She's French.

Is Charles in Chile?
No. He's in Chicago.

Do the children like chocolate?
Patricia likes chocolate.

31

Unit 3

Conversation:
Going to the dentist's office

Nancy: Are you going to see the dentist today?
Peter: Yes. I'm going to see him this afternoon.
Nancy: Is he going to fill some teeth?
Peter: No. He's only going to clean them.
Nancy: Are you afraid?
Peter: Of course not. I'm not afraid of the dentist. . . .

Are you going to see the dentist today?

Yes. I'm going to see him this afternoon.

Is he going to fill some teeth?

No. He's only going to clean them.

Are you afraid?

Of course not. I'm not afraid of the dentist. . . .

Adaptation

Construct two-line dialogues like the model. Use the cues.

1. dentist/today?   *Are you going to see the dentist today?*
   him/this afternoon.   *Yes. I'm going to see him this afternoon.*

   doctor/tomorrow? _____?
   her/tomorrow afternoon. _____.

   lawyer/tomorrow? _____?
   him/tomorrow morning. _____.

   psychiatrist/next week? _____?
   her/Monday morning. _____.

2. dentist/fill some teeth?   *Is the dentist going to fill some teeth?*
   He/clean them.   *No. He's only going to clean them.*

   teacher/give a test? _____?
   She/give a lecture. _____.

   hairdresser/cut your hair? _____?
   He/wash it. _____.

   doctor/operate on you? _____?
   She/examine me. _____.

Study 1

The future with **going to**: *I'm going to see him this afternoon.*

Notice the form of **be + going to + verb**:

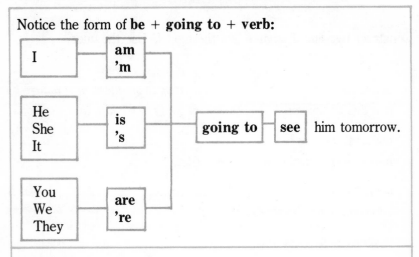

Going to + verb refers to an action in the future.

Use the appropriate form of **be (am, are, is) + going to +** simple verb.

Use the contractions in conversation.

For the future of **go**, the present progressive is usually used:
I'm going to Boston next week.

Notice these time expressions used with the future:

tomorrow
tomorrow morning
tomorrow afternoon
tomorrow evening
next week
next month
next year

Practice

1. Each person below is **going to** do something **tomorrow.** What is it?

She's going to see a movie tomorrow.

They're going to watch television tomorrow.

_____ .

_____ .

_____ .

_____ . 35

_____ .   _____ .

_____ .   _____ .

Study 2

The negative with **going to:** *He's not going to fill my teeth.*

Notice the negative forms of the verbs:

I'm not going to be here tomorrow.

We**'re not** going to play cards tonight.
We **aren't** going to play cards tonight.

He**'s not** going to take a vacation next year.
He **isn't** going to take a vacation next year.

Use the negative forms of **be** to form the negative with **going to.**

Is not is often contracted to **isn't.**

Are not is often contracted to **aren't.**

Practice

1. Make negative sentences with **going to.** Use the contractions **I'm not, you're not, he's not,** etc. Use the pictures as cues.

I'm going to talk.
▸ *I'm not going to listen.*

He's going to practice the piano.
▸ *He's not going to practice the guitar.*

We're going to paint the chairs.
▸ ‹‹‹

It's going to close at 5:30.
▸

I'm going to take a vacation in May.
▶

You're going to go to bed.
▶

She's going to buy a record.
▶

They're going to wash the dishes.
▶

2. Do Exercise 1 again, this time using the negative contractions **isn't** and **aren't** when possible.

I'm going to talk.

▶ *I'm not going to listen.*

He's going to practice the piano.
▶ *He isn't going to practice the guitar.*

Study 3

Yes/no questions with **going to:** *Are you going to see the dentist?*

Notice the order of the words:

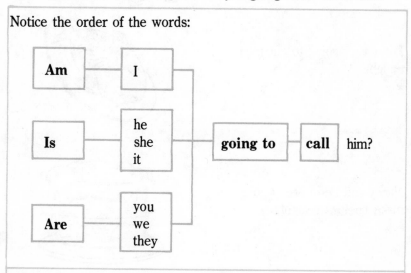

Am	I			
Is	he she it	going to	call	him?
Are	you we they			

Place the verb **be (am, are, is)** before the subject in questions with **going to.**

Practice

Form questions with **going to,** using the statements and the pictures below as cues.

Peter isn't going to see the
doctor this afternoon.
▶ *Is he going to see the dentist?*

Peter isn't going to take the
subway.
▶ *Is he going to take the bus?*

Peter isn't going to eat meat
tonight.
▶

Nancy and Peter aren't going to
make cookies tonight.
▶

Jean isn't going to see Mr.
Smith today.
▶

Mrs. Weber

Steve and Michael aren't going
to visit Jean today.
▶

Sally

I'm not going to call Helen tomorrow.

►

Sandra

We aren't going to give them a plant.

►

Study 4

Short answers to yes/no questions with **going to:** *Yes, he is. No, he's not.*

Notice the short answers to the questions:	
Are you going to be at the party?	**Yes, I am.**
Is the party going to be interesting?	**Yes, it is.**
Are Sandra and George going to be there?	**Yes, they are.**
Is Glen going to sing?	**No, he's not.**
	(No, he isn't.)
Are you going to play cards?	**No, we're not.**
	(No, we aren't.)
Are you going to stay late?	**No, I'm not.**

Affirmative short answers end with **am, is,** or **are.**
Negative short answers end with **not,** or with **isn't** or **aren't.**
Use contractions only in the negative.

Practice

Answer the questions according to the pictures. Use short answers.

Is Peter going to work this afternoon?
▶ *No, he's not.*

Are Nancy and Peter going to stay home tonight?
▶ *Yes, they are.*

Is Jean going to go ice-skating next winter?
▶

Are Jean and Sally going to work next weekend?
▶

Are you going to be at the beach tomorrow?
▶

Is it going to rain tomorrow?

Are we going to eat in a restaurant tonight?

Is Jean going to visit us next week?

Speak

1. **Nancy:** Are you going to drive to Boston tomorrow?
   Sarah: Yes. I'm going to leave at 6:00 in the morning.
   Nancy: Be very careful. It's snowing there.
   Sarah: Yes, I know. I'm going to drive very slowly.

2. **Sally:** Are you going to take a trip in August?
    Annette: Yes. I'm going to visit Denver.
    Sally: Are you going to call Ronald?
    Annette: No, I'm not. He isn't going to be there in August.

3. **Steve:** Is the store going to open soon?
    Douglas: Yes. It's going to open at nine o'clock.
    Steve: What time is it now?
    Douglas: It's a quarter to nine. Are you going to wait?
    Steve: No, I'm not. I don't have time.

Read

Nancy and Peter McCall like sports. In the summer they swim and in the winter they ski. They are planning a ski trip for this weekend, but they don't know about the weather. It's 7:30 now, and they are listening to the weather report on the radio. The weatherman is giving the weather for the weekend:

"Friday is going to be cold and cloudy, but it's not going to rain. The temperature is going to be in the thirties. It's going to snow Friday night and maybe Saturday morning. Saturday afternoon and Sunday are going to be clear, cold, and sunny."

Now Nancy and Peter are excited. The weather is going to be perfect for a ski trip. They are going to have a wonderful weekend in the mountains.

Answer the questions.

1. Are Nancy and Peter going to swim or ski this weekend?
2. Are they listening to the radio or watching television?
3. What time is it?
4. Is it going to rain on Friday?
5. Is it going to snow on Friday night or Saturday afternoon?
6. Is Sunday going to be cloudy or clear?
7. Do Nancy and Peter like the weather report?

Think

Janet is going to have a very busy weekend. What is she going to do?

Pronounce

Contrast [f] and [v].

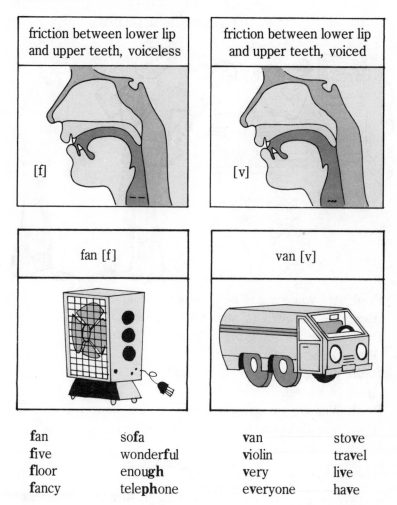

friction between lower lip and upper teeth, voiceless	friction between lower lip and upper teeth, voiced
[f]	[v]
fan [f]	van [v]

fan	sofa	van	stove
five	wonderful	violin	travel
floor	enough	very	live
fancy	telephone	everyone	have

The Fancy Van

Five of my friends have a wonderful van. When they travel, they always live in the van. There's enough room for everyone. There's a living room with a sofa, and a rug on the floor. There's a kitchen with a refrigerator, a stove, and a fan. It's definitely a very fancy van.

Unit 4

Conversation:
Taking a business trip

Paul: Are you going to be here next week?
Ben: No. I'm going to Atlanta on business.
Paul: When are you going to leave?
Ben: On Monday.
Paul: Where are you going to stay?
Ben: In a hotel.
Paul: Who are you going to see?
Ben: Jane Coleman. She's the manager there.

Are you going to be here next week?

No. I'm going to Atlanta on business.

When are you going to leave?

On Monday.

Where are you going to stay?

48   In a hotel.

Who are you going to see?

Jane Coleman. She's the manager there.

Adaptation

Construct two-line dialogues like the model. Use the cues.

1. you/be here next week?   *Are you going to be here next week?*
   to Atlanta on business.   *No. I'm going to Atlanta on business.*

   he/be here next week?   _____?
   to Mexico on vacation.   _____ . _____.

   they/be here Saturday?   _____?
   to Ohio for the weekend.   _____ . _____.

   she/be home next July?   _____?
   to Japan for the summer.   _____ . _____.

2. to leave?   *When are you going to leave?*
   On Monday.   *On Monday.*

   to arrive?   _____?
   On Tuesday morning.   _____.

   to have dinner?   _____?
   At eight o'clock.   _____.

   to see Jane?   _____?
   At 3:00 in the afternoon.   _____.

3. you/to stay?   *Where are you going to stay?*
   In a hotel.   *In a hotel.*

   she/to stay?   _____?
   At Jane's house.   _____.

   we/to eat?   _____?
   At a restaurant.   _____.   49

he/to live? _____?
In an apartment. _____

4. see?   *Who are you going to see?*
Jane Coleman. manager. *Jane Coleman. She's the manager there.*

talk to?   _____?
Vincent Marino. director._____ . _____ .

visit?   _____?
Sandra Wolf. accountant. _____ . _____ .

stay with?   _____?
Frank Martin. salesman. _____ . _____ .

Study 1

Information questions with **going to:** *When are you going to leave?*

Notice the formation of questions with **when, where, who(m),** and **how:**

Are you going to leave **on Sunday?** No, I'm not.

When are you going to leave?

Are you going to stay **in a motel?** No, I'm not.

Where are you going to stay?

Are you going to see **Howard Wolf?** No, I'm not.

Who(m) are you going to see?

Are you going to travel **by train?** No, I'm not.

How are you going to travel?

Use the appropriate question word at the beginning of the question. Use **who** in conversation and **whom** in formal writing.

Practice

1. Ben Miller is going to teach Paul and Susan Bruno a game. Answer the questions using the cues.

Who is Ben going to teach? (Paul and Susan)
▶ *He's going to teach Paul and Susan.*
What is he going to teach them? (tennis)
▶
Where are they going to play? (at the park)
▶
When are they going to play? (in the evening)
▶
When are they going to leave the park? (at ten o'clock)
▶
How are they going to go home? (by car)
▶

2. Form information questions based on the words in italics.

Is Ben going to take a vacation *in August?* No, he isn't.
▶ *When is he going to take a vacation?*

Is he going to travel *in Europe?* No, he isn't.
▶ *Where is he going to travel?*

Is he going to travel with *Paul?* No, he isn't.
▶

Are they going to travel *by bus?* No, they aren't.
▶

Are they going to buy *souvenirs?* No, they aren't.
▶

Are they going to visit *Sylvia?* No, they aren't.
▶

Is Sylvia going to be *home* this summer? No, she isn't.
▶

Are you going to visit your parents *this summer?* No, I'm not.
▶

3. What is Sally going to do each day next week?

Monday   Tuesday   Wednesday

Thursday   Friday   Saturday

When is she going to buy new boots?
► *She's going to buy new boots on Tuesday.*
When is she going to see the doctor?
►
When is she going to play volleyball?
►
When is she going to visit her parents?
►
When is she going to see a play?
►
When is she going to clean her apartment?
►
When is she going to drive to the mountains?
►

Sunday

Study 2

Short answers to information questions: *When are you going to leave?*
On Monday.

Notice the short answers:

When are you going to visit Colorado?
    Next August. (We're going to visit Colorado next August.)
Where are you going to stay?
    In Denver. (We're going to stay in Denver.)
How are you going to travel?
    By car. (We're going to travel by car.)

To make short answers to information questions, do not repeat any
words from the question. Answer only the question word:

        When? ► Next August.
        Where?► In Denver.
        How?   ► By car.

Practice

Answer the following questions according to the pictures. Use short answers.

Where are you going to have dinner?
▶ *At a restaurant.*

How are you going to the restaurant?
▶

When are you going to leave?
▶

Who are you going to have dinner with?
▶

Sally and Steve

What time are they going to arrive there?
▶

What are you going to have for dinner?
▶

What are you going to drink?

▶

Where are you going after
dinner?

▶

Speak

1. **Janet:** What are you going to do tonight?
   Joseph: I'm going to the movies.
   Janet: What are you going to see?
   Joseph: A new French film.
   Janet: Do you understand French?
   Joseph: No, I don't. But the film has subtitles.

55

2. **Paul:** Are you going to be home this afternoon?
   Susan: No. I'm going to play tennis.
   Paul: Where are you going to play?
   Susan: At the park.
   Paul: Who are you going to play with?
   Susan: Janice. She's a very good tennis player.

3. **Douglas:** Are you going to City College this summer?
   David: No, I'm not. I'm going to work full-time.
   Douglas: Where are you going to work?
   David: In a garage.
   Douglas: Don't you work in a garage now?
   David: Yes. But I only work part-time.

Read

Ben and Ruth Miller live in Chicago. Ruth is a chemist in a laboratory there, and Ben works in an advertising agency. Ben often takes business trips. When he takes a trip, Ruth stays in Chicago alone, but she is never bored. She finds many interesting things to do.

Next week Ben is going to Atlanta on business. He's going to leave on Monday and come home on Friday. Ruth is planning many activities for next week. She is going to do things that Ben doesn't enjoy. Ruth's favorite sport is volleyball, but Ben doesn't like it. So Ruth is going to play volleyball on Monday. She loves German food, but Ben doesn't. So on Tuesday she is going to eat in a German restaurant with some friends. On Wednesday she is going to a symphony concert. She enjoys classical music, but Ben only likes jazz. She likes foreign films too, but Ben prefers American films. Therefore, she is going to see a Japanese film on Thursday. On Friday she is going to meet Ben at the airport. They are going to eat in a Chinese restaurant. They like very different things, but they both love Chinese food.

Answer the questions.

1. Where do Ben and Ruth Miller work?
2. Who takes business trips?
3. Is Ruth bored when Ben takes a trip?

4. When is Ben going to leave for Atlanta?
5. What is Ruth going to do on Monday?
6. Where is she going to eat on Tuesday?
7. Does Ben enjoy classical music?
8. What is Ruth going to do on Thursday?
9. Does Ben like Chinese food?
10. Where are they going to eat on Friday?

Think

Ask questions about Ben Miller's trip to Atlanta. Answer them with short answers.

When is he going to leave?
On Monday.

How?

What time?

Where?

Who?

Where?

What?

What?

Pronounce

band [b]	exploded between lips, voiced
	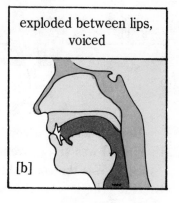

band	**b**reakfast	Ro**b**ert
bus	**b**read	clu**b**
beach	**b**ottle	a**b**out
big	**b**acon	num**b**er

I'm going to Colombia by bus.
The beaches there are beautiful.

Bill and Barbara are going to have a big breakfast.
Bill is going to buy bread and a bottle of milk.
Barbara is going to buy bacon and eggs.

Robert plays in a band at a club.
Band practice begins at six o'clock.

Unit 5

Conversation:
Going to a convention

Ben: Where were you last week?
Catherine: I was at a convention.
Ben: Was the convention here?
Catherine: No, it wasn't. It was in San Francisco.
Ben: How was it?
Catherine: It was boring. But the restaurants were fantastic!

Where were you last week?

I was at a convention.

Was the convention here?

No, it wasn't. It was in San Francisco.

How was it?

It was boring. But the restaurants were fantastic!

Adaptation

Construct two-line dialogues like the model. Use the cues.

1. last week?   *Where were you last week?*
   at a convention.   *I was at a convention.*

   yesterday?   _____?
   at a meeting.   _____.

   last night?   _____?
   at a party.   _____.

   yesterday afternoon? _____?
   at a soccer game.   _____.

2. convention/here?   *Was the convention here?*
   in San Francisco.   *No it wasn't. It was in San Francisco.*

   meeting/here?   _____?
   in Jane's office.   _____._____.

   party/here?   _____?
   at George's house. _____._____.

   soccer game/here?   _____?
   at the sports stadium. _____._____.

3. the convention?   *How was the convention?*
   boring.   *It was boring.*
   restaurants/fantastic. *But the restaurants were fantastic.*

   the meeting?   _____?
   interesting.   _____.
   problems/difficult. _____.

   the party?   _____?
   boring.   _____.
   food/delicious.   _____.

the soccer game?   _____ ?

exciting.   _____ .

weather/bad.   _____ .

Study 1

The past of **be:** *It was in San Francisco.*

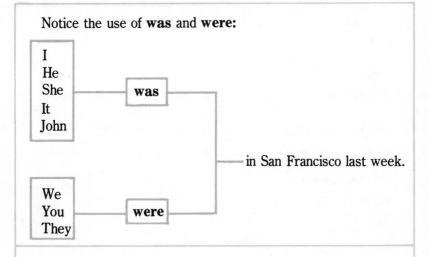

Notice the use of **was** and **were:**

I He She It John	**was**	
		in San Francisco last week.
We You They	**were**	

Use **was** with first person singular: **I.**

Use **was** with third person singular: **he, she, it.**

Use **were** with all other persons: **we, you, they.**

Notice these time expressions:

Present:	Past:
today	▶ **yesterday**
this morning	▶ **yesterday morning**
this afternoon	▶ **yesterday afternoon**
this evening	▶ **yesterday evening**
tonight	▶ **last night**

this week	▶ **last week**
this month	▶ **last month**
this year	▶ **last year**

Also: **three days ago**
two weeks ago
a year ago

Practice

Change each sentence to the past. Change both the verb and the time expression. Use the pictures as cues.

I am early this morning.
▶ *I was late yesterday morning.*

We are at a restaurant tonight.
▶ *We were at the movies last night.*

San Francisco

Catherine is in Chicago this week.
▶

They are lawyers this year.
▶

Mary is present today.
▶

You are sad this afternoon.
▶

She is fine this morning.
▶

They are in the mountains this weekend.
▶

The negative of **was** and **were**: *The convention wasn't here.*

Notice the formation of the negative:

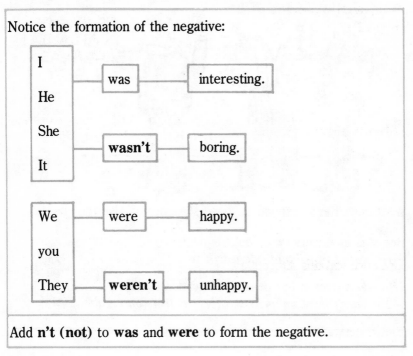

Add **n't (not)** to **was** and **were** to form the negative.

Practice

Paul, Ben, and Catherine work with Keith. Keith never agrees with the other people in the office. He always contradicts what they say.

What does Keith respond to these statements? Use the cues.

Ben was in Atlanta two weeks ago. (here)
▶ *He wasn't in Atlanta. He was here.*

Ben was there on business. (on vacation)
▶ *He wasn't there on business. He was there on vacation.*

Catherine was at a convention. (at home)
▶

The weather was good yesterday. (bad)
▶

Ben and Paul were early this morning. (late)
▶

Catherine was at the meeting today. (at a restaurant)
▶

The meeting was at nine o'clock. (eight o'clock)
▶

The meeting was interesting. (boring)
▶

Ben and Paul were happy after the meeting. (unhappy)
▶

Yes/no questions with the past of **be:** *Was the convention here?*

Notice the position of **was** and **were:**

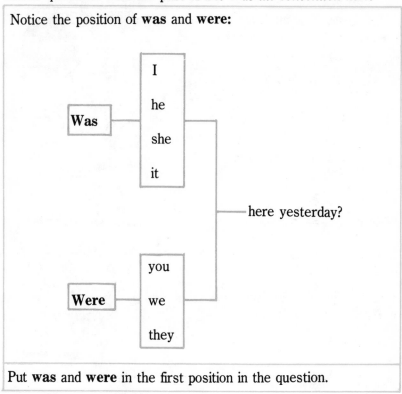

Put **was** and **were** in the first position in the question.

Practice

1. Ask each question and then answer it according to the picture.

Were Douglas and David in
college last year?
▶ *Yes. They were in college.*

Was David at home last night?
▶ *No. He was at the garage.*

Were Laura and Harold at a
party on Sunday?
▶

Were Laura and Sally at work
today?
▶

Was Nancy at the beach last
summer?
▶

Was Ben sick last week?
▶

Was Catherine at work
yesterday morning?

▶

Were you unhappy on Monday?

▶

2. Make questions in the past using **was** or **were**.

the play/last night?

Was the play last night?
No. It was last Friday.

Paul and Susan/there?

Were Paul and Susan there?
Yes. They were there.

the children/home?

_____ ?
No. They were at the play, too.

the play/at eight o'clock?

_____ ?
No. It was at 7:30.

you/late?

_____ ?
Yes. I was very late.

they/late?

_____ ?
No. They were early.

the play/interesting?

_____ ?
No. It was boring.

the play/long?

_____ ?
No. It was short.

69

Study 4

Short answers with the past of **be:** *Were you there? Yes, I was.*

Notice the short answers:

Were you at the convention?	**Yes, I was.**
Was the convention in Miami?	**No, it wasn't.**
Were the restaurants good?	**Yes, they were.**
Were the restaurants expensive?	**No, they weren't.**

Short answers end with **was, were, wasn't,** or **weren't.**

Practice

1. Answer the questions according to the pictures. Use short answers.

Were you at the picnic on Saturday?
▶ *Yes, I was.*

Was the weather nice?
▶ *No, it wasn't.*

Were Ben and Ruth there?
▶

Was the food delicious?
▶

Were the sandwiches cold?
▶

Was the coffee hot?
▶

Were the children happy?
▶

Were you hungry?
►

2. Give short answers in the affirmative and the negative, according to the pictures.

Were you and David in class?
► *I was, but David wasn't.*

Were David and Sally sick?
► *David was, but Sally wasn't.*

Were Sally and Laura at work?
►

Were the televisions and the radios expensive?
►

Were Catherine and Ben at the restaurant?

▶

Were the bananas and apples delicious?

▶

Were Paul and Susan happy?

▶

Study 5

Information questions with the past of **be:** *How was it?*

Notice the order of the words:

Was the meeting **last night?** No, it wasn't.

When was the meeting?

Was the discussion **interesting?** No, it wasn't.

How was the discussion?

Were Bill and Sue **there?** No, they weren't.

Where were Bill and Sue?

Place the question word in the first position, before **was** or **were.**

Practice

Give the information question that corresponds to the answer.

When was the rock concert?	The rock concert was last Saturday.
Where was the concert?	The concert was in the park.
_____ ?	The band was wonderful.
_____ ?	The band leader was excellent.
_____ ?	His name was Dale Jensen.
_____ ?	The new singer was in the hospital.
_____ ?	The new songs were beautiful.
_____ ?	Sally and Steve weren't there.
_____ ?	Bill's party was after the concert.
_____ ?	The party was fun.

Speak

Catherine: Were you and Ruth home last Sunday?

Ben: No, we weren't. We were at a photography exhibition.

Catherine: Where was it?

Ben: It was at the art museum.

Catherine: Was it interesting?

Ben: Yes, it was. The photographs were beautiful.

Ruth: What are you going to do tonight?

Catherine: I'm going to eat at the new Chinese restaurant.

Ruth: Really? I was there last night.

Catherine: How was the food?

Ruth: It was delicious. The vegetables were very fresh.

75

Paul: Was Catherine at Allen Martin's picnic?

Susan: No, she wasn't.

Paul: Where was she?

Susan: She was at home. There was a good movie on television.

Read

Catherine's vacation

Every summer Catherine has a two-week vacation. She usually travels during her vacation and visits new places. Last August she was in Europe. Europe was very beautiful, but her vacation wasn't very nice. She was on a tour of four countries, and she was in each country only three days. There were too many museums and monuments, and she was always in a hurry. She was on the train or on a bus almost every day. Also, she was alone, and the people on the tour weren't very friendly. After her vacation, she was tired and bored.

This summer she is going to have a very different vacation. She is going to travel to one country, and visit only one city. She is going to go with a friend. They aren't going to visit monuments and museums every day. They are going to choose a city on the ocean, and go to the beach sometimes. This year Catherine isn't going to feel tired after her vacation. She is going to feel relaxed and happy.

Answer the questions.

1. What does Catherine usually do on her vacation?
2. Where was she last August?
3. How was her vacation?
4. How were the people on the tour?
5. Is Catherine going to visit four countries this summer?
6. Is she going to go alone?
7. Are she and her friend going to visit museums every day?
8. How is she going to feel after her vacation?

Think

Catherine was at a convention in San Francisco last week. Ask her about her week, using the question word **how.** What does she answer?

How were the restaurants?
They were fantastic.

the food?

the weather?

the convention?

the people at the convention?

the hotel?

the night clubs?

Pronounce

Contrast [b] and [v].

band [b]	van [v]
	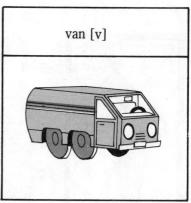

band	buy	van	give
blue	ball	Vivian	live
Beth	Bob	Victor	five
birthday	ribbon	velvet	seven

Beth and Victor have a blue van.
They live at seven seventy-seven Burk Boulevard.
Vivian and Bob sing in a band.
Beth has a birthday in five days.
Vivian is giving Beth a book on volleyball.
Victor is buying Beth a velvet ribbon.

Unit 6

Stanley Novak   Kate Ross

Stanley: Did you watch television last night?
Kate: Yes. I watched a program on Italy.
Stanley: Did they discuss Italian art?
Kate: No. They discussed Italian politics.
Stanley: Didn't you visit Italy last year?
Kate: Yes. I visited Rome and Florence.

Did you watch television last night?

Yes. I watched a program on Italy.

Did they discuss Italian art?

No. They discussed Italian politics.

Didn't you visit Italy last year?

Yes. I visited Rome and Florence.

Adaptation

Construct two-line dialogues like the model. Use the cues.

1. watch television last night? *Did you watch television last night?*
   a program on Italy. *Yes. I watched a program on Italy.*

   listen to the radio yesterday? _____?
   a program on education. _____ . _____ .

   practice the piano last night? _____?
   a piece by Bach. _____ . _____ .

   study geography last week? _____?
   a lesson on Africa. _____ . _____ .

2. they/discuss Italian art? *Did they discuss Italian art?*
   Italian politics. *No. They discussed Italian politics.*

   he/play tennis? _____?
   soccer. _____ . _____ .

   you/memorize the vocabulary? _____?
   the grammar. _____ . _____ .

   she/practice the guitar? _____?
   the violin. _____ . _____ .

3. visit Italy last year? *Didn't you visit Italy last year?*
   Rome and Florence. *Yes. I visited Rome and Florence.*

   visit South America last _____
   summer? _____?
   Chile and Argentina. _____ . _____ .

   study mathematics last _____
   year? _____?
   algebra and geometry. _____ . _____ .   81

learn a new language last
summer? _____
_____ ?
Greek. _____ . _____ .

Study 1

The regular past: *I listened. I watched. I visited.*

Notice the verb endings and their pronunciation:

| The past of | listen
open
live
play | is | **listened**
opened
lived
played | . | [d] |

| The past of | like
ask
practice
pronounce | is | **liked**
asked
practiced
pronounced | . | [t] |

| The past of | want
add
repeat
start | is | **wanted**
added
repeated
started | . | [id] |

The regular past ends in **-ed:** [d], [t], or [id].

Say [d] after a voiced final sound: **open►opened** [-nd]

Say [t] after a voiceless final sound: **like►liked** [-kt]

Say [id] after a final [t] or [d]:**want►wanted** [-tid]
                                  add►added [-did]

Practice

1. Write and pronounce the past form of these verbs according to the rules.

   Add **d** to the final letter **e**:

like	*liked*
memorize	*memorized*
practice	*practiced*
pronounce	*pronounced*

   Add **ed** to final consonants:

listen	*listened*
ask	*asked*
want	*wanted*
paint	*painted*

   Change **y** after a consonant to **i** and add **ed**:

study	*studied*
reply	*replied*
try	*tried*
cry	*cried*

2. a. Change to the past with the sound [t]. Use the expression **yesterday.**

   We walk to class every day.
   ▶ *We walked to class yesterday.*

   We discuss the grammar.
   ▶ *We discussed the grammar*

   We ask many questions.
   ▶ *We asked many question*

   We practice the dialogues.
   ▶ *We practiced the dialogues*

   We pronounce the new words.
   ▶ *We pronounced the new words.*

83

b. Change to the past with the sound [d]. Change the time expression to the corresponding past expression.

Bill listens to the program every night.
▶ *Bill listened to the program last night.*

He remembers my birthday every year.
▶ He remembered my birthday last ~~every~~ year.

He plays soccer every day.
▶ He played soccer last year.

He stays at home every Sunday.
▶ He stayed at home last sunday

He opens his mail in the morning.
▶ He opened his mail in the morning

c. Change to the past with the sound [id]. Change the time expression to the corresponding past expression.

The game starts at 1:00 on Saturday.
▶ *The game started at 1:00 last Saturday.*
the game start
Mary wants a ticket this week.
▶ Mary wanted a ticket last week

We visit Mary on Wednesday.
▶ We visited mary on

John paints a picture every weekend.
▶

I need new shoes every year.
▶

3. Describe the actions. Use the past and add **last Saturday.** Use the pictures as cues.

They studied the lesson last Saturday.

We _____ (look).

She _____ (practice).

I _____ (ask).

Ben _____ (play).

They _____ (paint).

Janet

Steve _____ (talk).

He _____ (watch).

Yes/no questions in the past tense: *Did you watch television last night?*

Notice the questions in the present and the past:

Present:

Past:

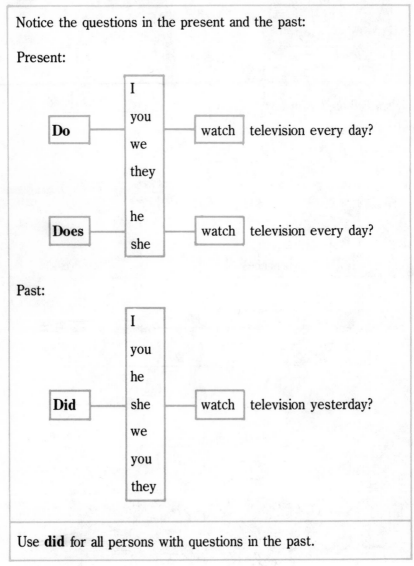

Use **did** for all persons with questions in the past.

Practice

1. Ask yes/no questions in the past using the appropriate past expression.

I work hard almost every day.
▶ *Did you work hard yesterday?*

We clean the house almost every Saturday.
▶ *Did you clean the house last Saturday?*

He washes his clothes almost every Saturday.
▶

Ben plays tennis with Ruth almost every weekend.
▶

Ben practices almost every day.
▶

Ben and Ruth visit their parents almost every Sunday.
▶

We discuss politics almost every night.
▶

I remember my medicine almost every day.
▶

I arrive late almost every morning.
▶

2. Ask yes/no questions using the cues, and then answer them according to the pictures.

they/play the piano?  *Did they play the piano?*
No. They played the guitar.

he/study English?

Did he study English?
No. He studied Russian.

he/visit Spain?

England

_____ ?
___ . _____ .

they/dance slowly?

_____ ?
___ . _____ .

he/clean the wall?

_____ ?
___ . _____ .

she/wash the table?

_____ ?
___ . _____ .

you/paint the bedroom?  _____ ?
_____ . _____ .

you/watch the news?  _____ ?
_____ . _____ .

Speak

1. **Janet:** Did you watch TV yesterday?
   Michael: Yes. I watched it in the evening.
   Janet: Did you listen to the news?
   Michael: No. Was it important?
   Janet: Yes, it was. They talked about the mail strike.

89

huelga

2. Stanley: Hello, Kate. Where were you on Saturday?
     Kate: At home. I played cards with Dick.
Stanley: Did you play cards all day?
     Kate: No. I listened to music in the evening.
Stanley: What did you do on Sunday?
     Kate: On Sunday I . . .

Continue the dialogue with the verbs below:

dance	practice	discuss
study	visit	play
watch	talk	paint
work	walk	stay
clean	wash	call

Read

Catherine Wells was at home on Monday night, and she watched an interesting television program. The program was about California history. It was a long program. It started at nine o'clock and ended at ten thirty. Her father loves California, so Catherine called her father and explained the program to him. Mr. Wells was very interested in it. The television station repeated the program on Sunday afternoon. Catherine visited her father on Sunday, and they watched the program together. Mr. Wells liked it very much.

Answer the questions.

1. Who watched the program on Monday night?
2. Was the program about science?
3. Did it end at nine o'clock?
4. Who was interested in the program?
5. Did they repeat the program on Saturday or Sunday?
6. Who watched it on Sunday afternoon?
7. Did Mr. Wells like it?

Think

Kate Ross and her husband Dick visited Italy last year. Ask yes/no questions about their trip using the pictures below.

Did they study their guide book?
Yes. They studied it.

she/visit

she/look

they/dance

he/talk

she/ask

they/walk

they/listen

Pronounce

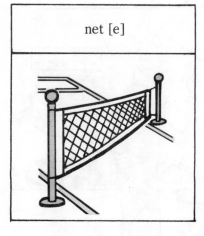

net [e]

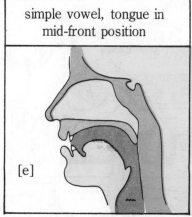

simple vowel, tongue in mid-front position

[e]

net	get	friend	address
pen	bed	Helen	elephant
tell	then	French	excellent
bread	tent	when	expensive
desk	cents	seventy	restaurant

Did you play tennis with your friends?
Yes. I played yesterday.
Did Helen play with Ben?
Yes. Her tennis is excellent.

How was the French restaurant?
It was excellent, but it was expensive.
When were you there?
Last Wednesday.
Tell me the address.
Eleven-seventy Kent Street.

Unit 7

Stanley Novak   Dick Ross

Stanley: Did you go to the movies last Saturday?

Dick: No. I went to the football game.

Stanley: Did our team win?

Dick: No, we didn't. We lost.

Stanley: Did we lose by much?

Dick: We lost by twelve points.

Stanley: Oh. I'm glad I didn't go.

Did you go to the movies last Saturday?

No. I went to the football game.

Did our team win?

No, we didn't. We lost.

Did we lose by much?

We lost by twelve points.

Oh. I'm glad I didn't go.

94

Adaptation

Construct two-line dialogues like the model, using the cues.

1. go to the movies?   *Did you go to the movies?*
   went to the football game. *No. I went to the football game.*

   see Jane and Bill there?   _____?
   saw Sarah and Bob.   _____. _____.

   eat at the stadium?   _____?
   ate at home.   _____. _____.

   drink soda?   _____?
   drank orange juice.   _____. _____.

2. our team/win?   *Did our team win?*
   lost.   *No, we didn't. We lost.*

   the game/begin on time? _____?
   began late.   _____. _____.

   you/watch the game?   _____?
   slept.   _____. _____.

   you/have a good time?   _____?
   had a terrible time.   _____. _____.

3. we/lose by much?   *Did we lose by much?*
   lost by twelve points.   *We lost by twelve points.*

   you/sleep much?   _____?
   slept for an hour.   _____.

   he/eat much?   _____?
   ate three sandwiches.   _____.

   they/read much?   _____?
   read two books.   _____.   95

Study 1

The irregular past: *I went to the football game.*

Learn these irregular past forms:

The past of ... is ...

speak	**spoke**
write	**wrote**
tell	**told**
eat	**ate**
give	**gave**
sing	**sang**
drink	**drank**
begin	**began**
have	**had**
take	**took**
understand	**understood**
see	**saw**
buy	**bought**
get	**got**
win	**won**
lose	**lost**
go	**went**
leave	**left**
sleep	**slept**
read [iy]	**read [e]**

Practice

1. Answer the questions in the past according to the pictures.

Did you leave work at 5:00 or
5:30?
▶ *I left work at 5:00.*

Did you go home or go out?
▶ *I went out.*

Did you go to the concert or
the game?
▶

Did our team win or lose?
▶

Did you eat in a restaurant or
at home?
▶

Did you have a big dinner or
a sandwich?
▶

Did you get home early or
late?
▶

Did you go to sleep or read?
▶

Did you sleep well or badly?
▶

Did you get up early or late?
▶

2. What did these people do after work last night?

go

He went home.

see

They saw a movie.

drink

eat

write

go

buy

read

99

sang

sleep

Study 2

Negative statements in the past: *We didn't win.*

Notice the verb form in the negative and the affirmative:

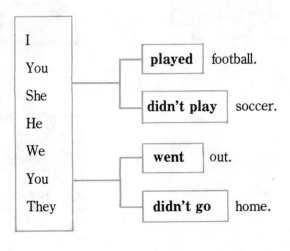

To form the past negative, use **didn't** and the simple form of the verb. (The simple form of **played** is **play;** the simple form of **went** is **go.**)

Didn't is the contraction of **did not.**

Practice

Complete each sentence using the negative form of the verb.

Kate and Dick visited Italy,
but Stanley didn't visit Italy.

Kate spoke Italian,
but Dick didn't speak Italian.

Kate watched a program on Italy,
but Stanley _didn't watch a program on Italy_ .

Catherine went to San Francisco,
but Ben and Paul _didn't go to San francisco_ .

Catherine took a vacation in Europe,
but Ben and Ruth _didn't take a vacation in Europe_ .

Ben and Ruth ate in a Chinese restaurant,
but Paul and Susan _didn't eat in a Chinese restaurant_ .

Ben took a business trip,
but Ruth _didn't take a business trip_ .

Ben saw Jane Coleman,
but Catherine _didn't see Jane Coleman_ .

Dick went to the game,
but Stanley _didn't go to the game_ .

Janet listened to the news,
but Michael _didn't listen to the news._ . 101

Study 3

Short answers with **did** and **didn't**: *Yes, I did. No, I didn't.*

Notice the negative and affirmative short answers in the past:

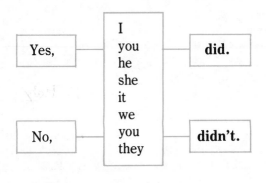

Did and **didn't** complete the short answers in the past tense.

Practice

Answer according to the pictures. Give short answers.

Did you read the paper on Sunday?
▶ *Yes, I did.*

Did he stay home on Saturday night?
▶ *No, he didn't.*

Did you speak to Jane Coleman?
▶ Yes, I did.

Jane Coleman

Did they play volleyball?
▶ no, they didn't

Did Richard call his friend?
▶ yes, He did.

Did I give you my book?
▶ yes, you did.

Did he get up at 6:30?
▶ no, He didn't.

103

Did Janet like the cat?
▶

Did Philip like class?
▶

Did Jean eat fish?
▶

Speak

1. **Mr. Novak:** Did you go to the game today?
   Fred: Yes, I did.
   Mr. Novak: Did you have a good time?
   Fred: Yes. It was exciting. Our team won by one point.

2. **Dolores:** Did you have a nice Sunday?
   Howard: Yes. I read the paper and went to church.
   Dolores: Did you go out in the evening?
   Howard: No. I stayed home. Did you?
   Dolores: Yes, I did. I went to the movies.

3. **Dolores:** Did you eat at home on Friday?
   Howard: No. I ate dinner at a Spanish restaurant.
   Dolores: Did you understand the menu?
   Howard: Of course I did. I know Spanish.
   Dolores: Did you speak Spanish to the waiter?
   Howard: No. I spoke English. I don't speak Spanish very well. 105

Read

Steve and Michael at the museum

Steve and I got up at seven o'clock yesterday. We had a big breakfast. Then we took the bus downtown and went to an art museum. It opened at nine o'clock. We saw some beautiful paintings. We had a guide, and he explained everything to us. I liked all the art, but Steve didn't like the modern art very much. I bought copies of two paintings. I'm going to put them on the wall of my bedroom.

At one o'clock we were hungry, and we ate sandwiches in the museum cafeteria. I was thirsty, so I drank milk with my sandwich. After lunch we took a walk in the park. Then we went home at five o'clock. We were very tired, but we had a good time. Next week we are going to visit the science museum. It is very interesting too.

Answer the questions.

1. Did they get up early or late?
2. Did they have a small breakfast?
3. Did they take the subway or the bus?
4. Did they see paintings or sculpture?
5. Did Steve like the modern art?
6. Did Michael buy paintings at the museum?
7. Did they have lunch at the museum?
8. What are they going to do next week?

Think

1. This is Howard's appointment book for last week. What did he do each day?

MONDAY
Write to Henry

TUESDAY
play cards

WEDNESDAY
buy a new shirt

THURSDAY
Call Dolores

FRIDAY
eat at the new Spanish restaurant

SATURDAY
go to the football game

SUNDAY
go to church

2. Write a letter to a friend. Write your activities for the week day by day. Follow the example below:

Dear _____,

    Last week was a busy week for me. I wrote two letters on Monday. On Tuesday John and I went to the football game. . . .

Pronounce

nut [ə]

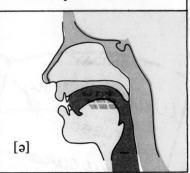

simple vowel, tongue in mid-central position, relaxed

[ə]

funny	monkey	does	dull
hungry	mother	doesn't	cover
nuts	some	young	ugly
lunch	month	country	judge

Was the zoo interesting?
Yes! The monkeys were funny.
They were very hungry.
Mother gave them some nuts for lunch.

aburrido = bored

Is the book dull?
No, it's not.
Well, the cover is ugly.
Don't judge a book by its cover.

juzgar (wanted/fusgado)

Unit 8
Conversation:
Discussing a recent event

Mrs. Ross   Fred Novak

Mrs. Ross: What did you do last weekend?
    Fred: I went to the circus with Mary Ann.
Mrs. Ross: The circus! When did it come?
    Fred: It came last Thursday.
Mrs. Ross: How was it?
    Fred: It was excellent. We enjoyed it very much.
Mrs. Ross: What did you like?
    Fred: We liked everything: the clowns, the acrobats,
              the elephants, and the lions.

What did you do last weekend?

I went to the circus with Mary Ann.

The circus! When did it come?

It came last Thursday.

How was it?

109

It was excellent. We enjoyed it very much.

What did you like?

We liked everything: the clowns, the acrobats,

the elephants, and the lions.

Adaptation

Construct two-line dialogues like the model using the cues.

1. you/last weekend?   *What did you do last weekend?*
   went to the circus with   *I went to the circus with Mary Ann.*
   Mary Ann.

   she/last Sunday?   _____ ?
   visited a museum with   _____
   Bill and Bob.   _____ .

   they/last week?   _____ ?
   saw a play with Richard. _____ .

   he/last summer?   _____ ?
   worked in a restaurant. _____ .

2. come?   *When did it come?*
   last Thursday.   *It came last Thursday.*

   start?   _____ ?
   eight o'clock.   _____ .

   end?   _____ ?
   midnight.   _____ .

   you/get home?   _____ ?
   1:00 in the morning.   _____ .

3. the circus?   *How was the circus?*
   excellent. enjoyed.   *It was excellent. We enjoyed it very much.*

   the clowns?   _____ ?
   funny. enjoyed.   _____ . _____ .

   the food?   _____ ?
   delicious. enjoyed.   _____ . _____ .

   the animals?   _____ ?
   interesting. enjoyed. _____ . _____ .

4. like?   *What did you like?*
   the clowns, the acrobats, *We liked everything: the clowns, the acro-*
   the elephants, and the *bats, the elephants, and the lions.*
   lions.

   visit?   _____ ?
   the museums, the the- _____
   aters, the stores,   _____
   and the restaurants   _____ .

   eat?   _____ ?
   the soup, the salad,   _____
   the fish, and the rice. _____ .

   buy?   _____ ?
   the dresses, the hats, _____
   the coats, and the shoes. _____ .

Study 1

Information questions in the past: *What did you like?*

Notice the formation of information questions with **did:**

Did you see the game? No, we didn't.

What did you see?

Did you see **John?** No, we didn't.

Who(m) did you see?

Did you go **to the city?** No, we didn't.

Where did you go?

Did it begin **at six?** No, it didn't.

When did it begin?

Did it begin **with music?** No, it didn't.

How did it begin?

Use the verb forms and word order for yes/no questions, and place the appropriate question word at the beginning of the question.

Practice

1. Answer the questions according to the picture.

Where did Fred go?
▶ *He went to the circus.*

Who did he go with?
▶ *He went with Mary Ann.*

When did the show begin?
▶

How were the clowns, funny or dull?
▶

Where was the lion, in the ring or in the cage?
▶

Where was the lion tamer?
▶

Where were the horses?
▶

What did Fred eat?
▶

2. Construct short dialogues like the examples: Give a negative short answer to each question. Then ask an appropriate information question and answer it according to the pictures.

Did you go *to the game?*
No, I didn't.
Where did you go?
I went to the circus.

Did Kate and Dick see *the circus?*
No, they didn't.
What did they see?
They saw a play.

Did the play end *at ten?*
_____ .
_____ ?
_____ .

Did they eat *at the restaurant?*
_____ .
_____ ?
_____ .

Did they have *ice cream* for dessert?
_____ .
_____ ?
_____ .

Did he eat the cake *with a spoon?*

_____ .
_____ ?
_____ .

Did Fred talk to *Dick Ross?*

_____ .
_____ ?
_____ .

Kate Ross

Study 2

Information questions about the verb phrase: *What did you do last weekend?*

Notice the use of **do** in these questions:

Did you stay home?   No, I didn't.
What did you do?

Did you play basketball?   No, I didn't.
What did you do?

Did you work all day?   No, I didn't.
What did you do all day?

Use **what + do** for information questions about the verb phrase:
stay home, play basketball, work.

115

Practice

1. Construct short dialogues like the examples. Make questions with **what + do.** Use the pictures as cues.

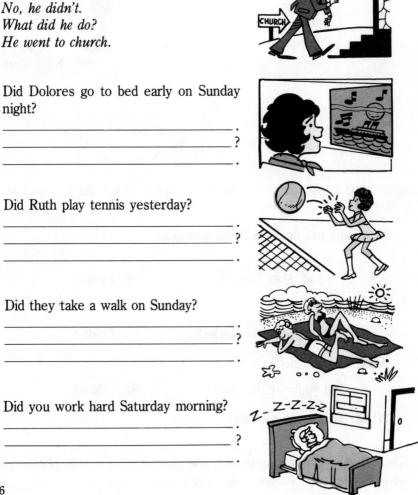

Did you go to the beach last weekend?
No, I didn't.
What did you do?
I went to the mountains.

Did Howard stay home on Sunday?
No, he didn't.
What did he do?
He went to church.

Did Dolores go to bed early on Sunday night?

_____ .
_____ ?
_____ .

Did Ruth play tennis yesterday?

_____ .
_____ ?
_____ .

Did they take a walk on Sunday?

_____ .
_____ ?
_____ .

Did you work hard Saturday morning?

_____ .
_____ ?
_____ .

2. What did these people do on Sunday? Ask a question with **what** + **do** for each picture, and then answer it.

What did Fred do?
He went to the circus.

What did Kate Ross do?
She played tennis.

Dolores

Bob

Ben and Ruth

Catherine

Howard

Steve and Michael

117

Study 3

In, on: *The lion was in the cage.*

Discover the meanings of **in** and **on** by looking at the pictures:

The water is **in** the pitcher.

The pitcher is **on** the table.

Practice

Construct sentences like the model. Use the pictures as cues.

cat/bag.
▶ *The cat is in the bag.*

book/floor.
▶ *The book is on the floor.*

picture/wall.
▶

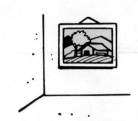

shoes/box.
▶

fish/water.
▶

apples/basket.
▶

woman/living room.
▶

watch/table.

▶

Think

The clown put the flower in the vase, but the vase was on a very tall stand. How did he put the flower in the vase?

Use this vocabulary:

first, then
put, get up, fall down

First, he put the box on the trunk. Then, he put the chair. . . .

Speak

1.   **Fred:** How was the circus last night?
  Francis: It was funny. I really enjoyed the clowns.
      Fred: Did you like the lion tamer?
  Francis: Yes, I did. He was very brave.
      Fred: How did you like the lions?
  Francis: I didn't like them very much. I was afraid of them.

2.   **Kate:** What did you do last Sunday?
  Sylvia: I rode my bicycle. What did you do?
  Kate: I went to the office.

Sylvia: The office! What did you do there?

Kate: I wrote a report.

Sylvia: Did you work all day?

Kate: No. I played tennis in the afternoon.

Read

Absent-minded Mr. Newton

Mr. Newton wasn't a genius, and he wasn't a fool; he was absent-minded. One day he left work at the usual time, six o'clock. He felt very cold outside, and he didn't understand . . . but of course! He didn't have his coat—it was in the office. He went back to the office and got his coat. On the way home he went to the club. He usually saw his friends there on Tuesday. That day he didn't see them. They weren't there. Then he remembered: It wasn't Tuesday; it was Wednesday!

122

Mr. Newton arrived home at eight o'clock, and his family wasn't home! He waited, and he worried about them. He didn't eat. He wasn't hungry. Mr. Newton called a friend and told him, "My family isn't home." Then he remembered: The children play tennis on Wednesday, and their mother takes them to the park. Today isn't Tuesday; it's Wednesday.

Mr. Newton wasn't worried then; he was hungry. He ate some bread, soup, meat, and potatoes, and he drank some milk. After supper he fell asleep. Later, Mr. Newton heard thieves enter the house. They didn't make much noise, and they didn't turn on the lights. Mr. Newton was very afraid, and he didn't move. He took a chair in his hand. He stood up slowly. He lifted the chair in the air, and then he heard:

"Father! What are you doing?"

Now he remembered. It wasn't thieves. It was his family!

Answer the questions.

1. Was Mr. Newton a genius or a fool?
2. When does he usually leave work?
3. How did he feel outside?
4. Where was his coat?
5. Did he see his friends at the club?
6. Was it Tuesday?
7. Was his family home at eight o'clock?
8. Who did Mr. Newton call?
9. What did he tell his friend?
10. Where was his family?
11. What did he do after supper?
12. What did he hear later?
13. What did Mr. Newton do with the chair?
14. Did thieves enter the house?

Pronounce

Contrast [e] and [ə].

net [e]	nut [ə]
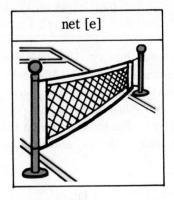	

desk	pencil	does	lunch
slept	address	come	subject
question	invent	club	number
medicine	chemistry	brother	discuss
engineer	went	was	London
letter	friend	subway	study

My brother Edmund is an engineer. He went to London for ten days last month. He was studying the subway system there. He went to a subway station with three women and seven men.

Who were the ten people at the subway station with Edmund? They were engineers. He discussed the system with them.

Edmund wrote a letter to his friends yesterday. He thanked them for their help.

Unit 9

Conversation:
Seeing a friend unexpectedly

Beth: What were you doing at the courthouse yesterday?
Eve: I was waiting for my uncle.
Beth: What was he doing there?
Eve: He was working. He's a lawyer. Were you there, too?
Beth: Yes, I was.
Eve: What were you doing there?
Beth: I was getting a driver's license.

What were you doing at the courthouse yesterday?

I was waiting for my uncle.

What was he doing there?

He was working. He's a lawyer. Were you there, too?

Yes, I was.

What were you doing there?

I was getting a driver's license.

125

Adaptation

Construct two-line dialogues like the model, using the cues.

1. you/courthouse?   *What were you doing at the courthouse?*
   waiting for my uncle. *I was waiting for my uncle.*

   he/post office?   _____?
   buying stamps.   _____.

   they/bus station?   _____?
   waiting for Jean.   _____.

   you/police station?   _____?
   looking for my wallet. _____.

   she/library?   _____?
   reading a magazine.   _____.

2. your uncle/there?   *What was your uncle doing there?*
   working. lawyer.   *He was working. He's a lawyer.*

   your aunt/at the hospital?_____?
   working. doctor.   _____. _____.

   your cousins/on the   _____
     boat?   _____?
   fishing. fishermen.   _____. _____.

   your brothers/at the   _____
     store?   _____?
   selling books. salesmen. _____. _____.

   your sister/at the game? _____?
   taking pictures.   _____
126   photographer.   _____.

3. you/there?   *Were you there, too?*
   Yes,   *Yes, I was.*

   you/at the post office?   _____?
   No,   _____.

   they/at the bus station?   _____?
   Yes,   _____.

   they/at the hospital?   _____?
   No,   _____.

   she/at the football game? _____?
   No,   _____.

Study 1

Past progressive form: *He was working.*

Notice the use of **was** and **were** with the **-ing** form of the verb:

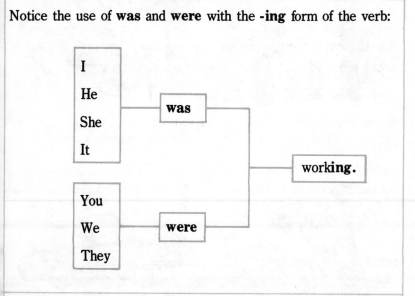

To form the past progressive, use the past of **be** (**was** or **were**)
with the **-ing** form of the main verb.

The past progressive tense indicates activity in progress in the past. Contrast the simple past tense and the past progressive tense:

He worked last night.

He worked: activity completed in the past.

I called him, but he wasn't home: He was working last night.

He was working: activity in progress in the past.

Practice

1. At five o'clock there was a big rainstorm. What were these people doing at five o'clock? Put the verbs in the past progressive tense.

Jim and Fred/talk
▶ *Jim and Fred were talking.*

Eve/read
▶ *Eve was reading a book.*

Mary Ann/take

Beth/drive

▶

Kate and Dick/play
▶

Stanley/wash
▶

Sylvia/ride
▶

Howard and Dolores/walk
▶

2. Ann Novak called her husband Stanley at eight o'clock last night. Everyone in the Novak family was doing something different. What were they doing?

129

Study 2

Negative past progressive form: *I wasn't waiting.*

Notice the formation of the negative with the past progressive tense:

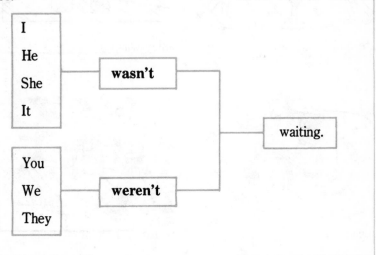

To form the negative of the past progressive tense, change the past of **be (was, were)** to the negative **(wasn't, weren't).**

Practice

Change each sentence to the negative, using the new object.

I was opening the door.
▶ *I wasn't opening the window.*

Stanley   Dick

They were waiting for Stanley.
▶ *They weren't waiting for Dick.*

She was reading the paper.
▶

I was listening to the news.
▶

You were driving slowly.
▶

She was drinking tea.
▶

They were looking at the sculpture.
▶

She was playing volleyball.
▶

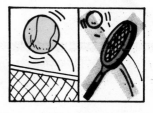

Study 3

Yes/no questions in the past progressive: *Was he eating?*

Notice the order of the words:

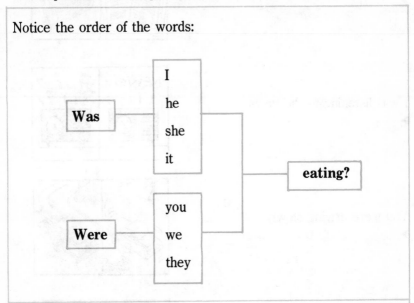

Put **was** or **were** in the first position in yes/no questions in the past progressive.

Practice

Change the sentence to a yes/no question using the new object.

Eve was helping her friend.
▶ *Was she helping Beth?*

Beth

They were visiting a museum.
▶ *Were they visiting the science museum?*

She was talking to a little boy.
▶

Fred

I was traveling in Mexico.
▶

We were eating dinner.
▶

He was having breakfast.
▶

They were watching television.
▶

133

I was listening to the radio.
▶

She was buying a present for her father.
▶

Study 4

Short answers to yes/no questions in the past progressive: *Yes, I was.*
No, I wasn't.

Notice the short answer forms:

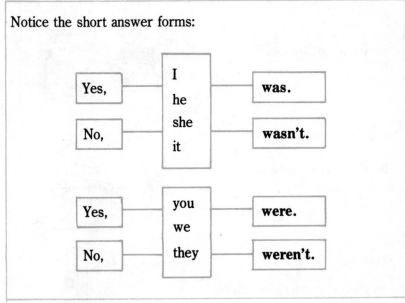

The past form of **be** (**was, wasn't, were,** or **weren't**) completes the short answers.

Practice

Answer the questions according to the pictures. Give short answers.

Was he studying?
▶ *Yes, he was.*

Was he studying at the library?
▶ *No, he wasn't.*

Was she going to San Francisco?
▶

Was she going by bus?
▶

Were they drinking wine?
▶

Were they having dinner?
▶

Was he sitting in the chair?
▶

Was he reading?
▶

Were you eating pizza?
▶

Were you drinking soda?
▶

135

Study 5

Information questions with the past progressive: *What was he doing?*

Notice the order of the words:

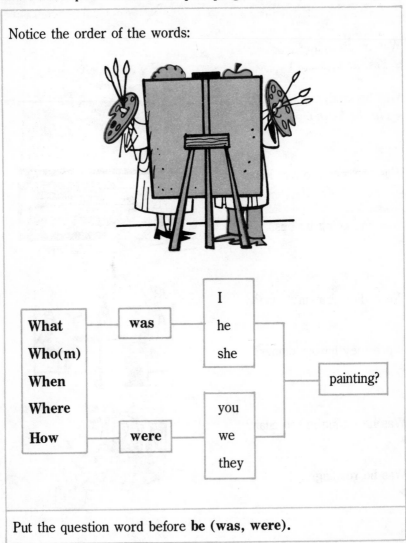

Put the question word before **be (was, were)**.

Practice

1. Howard had lunch with Beth and Eve yesterday. Their appointment was for twelve o'clock, but Howard arrived at a quarter after twelve. What were the people at the restaurant doing when Howard arrived?

What were Beth and Eve doing, eating or waiting?
▶ *They were waiting.*

Where were they sitting, in the kitchen or the dining room?
▶

Who were they talking to, the waiter or the waitress?
▶

What was the waiter doing, working or eating?
▶

Where was the waiter working, in the kitchen or the dining room?
▶

Where was the cook working?
▶

What was the cook preparing, meat or fish?
▶

2. Construct short dialogues like the examples below. Answer both the yes/no questions and the information questions with short answers.

Were Beth and Eve waiting *for Dolores?*
No, they weren't.
Who were they waiting for?
Howard.

Was the waiter *eating?*
No, he wasn't.
What was he doing?
Working.

Were you having lunch *at the restaurant?*
_____ .
_____ ?
_____ .

Were you eating *fish?*
_____ .
_____ ?
_____ .

Were you having lunch with *Sylvia?*
_____ .
_____ ?
_____ .

Was Kate eating *with her hands?*

_____ .
_____ ?
_____ .

Were Stanley and Dick *working?*

_____ .
_____ ?
_____ .

Speak

1. **Eve:** Did you go out for coffee after the game?
   Beth: No. I stayed at the hockey rink for an hour.
   Eve: What were you doing?
   Beth: I was waiting for my brother.

Eve: What was he doing?
Beth: He was interviewing a player.
Eve: Is he a newspaper reporter?
Beth: No. He's a reporter for a television station.

2. **Stanley:** Do you know Mary?
   Kate: Yes, I do.
   Stanley: When did you meet her?
   Kate: Last August.
   Stanley: How did you meet her?
   Kate: Sylvia introduced us.
   Stanley: Where did you meet her?
   Kate: In Florida. We were all on vacation there.

Read

John read a science magazine yesterday. He read about the discovery of penicillin:

"Doctor Alexander Fleming was studying bacteria in London in 1928. One day he was working in his office. He was looking at germs, and by accident he noticed something very interesting: a mold was growing in the bottles, and the bacteria were dying. "Dr. Fleming visited a little girl. She was very sick. She had the same germs in her body. He thought about the mold and the germs in his office. Was the mold in the bottles killing the germs? Dr. Fleming prepared some medicine with the mold, and he gave it to the girl. It made her well. He named the mold penicillin. Dr. Fleming's discovery is now helping millions of people in the world. They are getting well with penicillin."

Answer the questions.

1. What did John read about yesterday?
2. What was Dr. Fleming doing in 1928?
3. Where was he studying?
4. What was growing in the bottles?
5. What did the little girl have in her body?
6. What did Dr. Fleming give her?
7. What was killing the bacteria in the bottles?
8. What did Dr. Fleming name the mold?
9. Who is using penicillin now?

Think

What was Dr. Fleming doing in 1928?

Pronounce

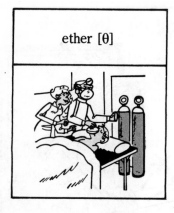

ether [θ]

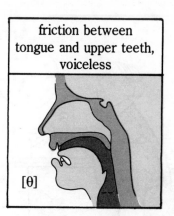

friction between tongue and upper teeth, voiceless

[θ]

think	Kathleen	thirsty	mouth
three	Elizabeth	theater	tooth
thirteen	Ethel	Thursday	month
thirty	Martha	thanks	Kenneth

Kathleen's birthday is next Thursday.
She is going to be thirteen.

Elizabeth and Martha aren't home.
They're studying math at Ethel's.

When did Kenneth go to the theater?
Last month, I think.

Are there thirty-two teeth in your mouth?
I think there are only thirty.

Unit 10

Conversation:
Arriving late for work

Mr. Smith   Albert

Mr. Smith: Aren't you late for work?
    Albert: Yes, I am. I had a little accident.
Mr. Smith: Really? What happened to you?
    Albert: I fell down and hurt my knee.
Mr. Smith: How did that happen?
    Albert: I don't know. I think I was running too fast.
Mr. Smith: Running? Were you in a hurry?
    Albert: Yes, I was. I was late for work.

> Aren't you late for work?
>
> Yes, I am. I had a little accident.
>
> Really? What happened to you?
>
> I fell down and hurt my knee.
>
> How did that happen?
>
> I don't know. I think I was running too fast.

Running? Were you in a hurry?

Yes, I was. I was late for work.

Adaptation

Construct two-line dialogues like the model. Use the cues.

1. you/late for work?   *Aren't you late for work?*
   Yes,   *Yes, I am.*

   he/late for school?   _____ ?
   Yes,   _____ .

   she/tired?   _____ ?
   Yes,   _____ .

   they/bored?   _____ ?
   Yes,   _____ .

2. to you?   *What happened to you?*
   knee.   *I fell down and hurt my knee.*

   to her?   _____ ?
   arm.   _____ .

   to him?   _____ ?
   leg.   _____ .

   to me?   _____ ?
   head.   _____ .

3. running too fast.   *I think I was running too fast.*
   in a hurry?   *Running? Were you in a hurry?*

   eating too much.   _____ .
   hungry?   _____ ? _____ ? 145

drinking too much.   _____ .

thirsty.   _____ ? _____ ?

crying too loud.   _____ .

unhappy?   _____ ? _____ ?

Study 1

General questions with **happen:** *What happened to you?*

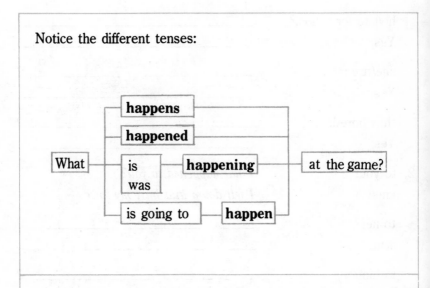

Notice the different tenses:

What	happens / happened		at the game?
	is / was	happening	
	is going to	happen	

Use **what** plus the verb **happen** to ask general questions about events. **What** is the subject of the question.

A question with **happen** is asking for complete information, so answer it with a complete sentence:

What happened at the game?
Philadelphia lost by one point.

Practice

Answer the questions according to the pictures.

1. What was happening?

a. *A boy was running.*

b. _____.

c. _____.

d. _____.

e. _____.

2. What happened?

f. came

e. called, ambulance

d. stopped, car

a. hit, boy

b. fell down

c. helped, boy

a. *The car hit the boy.*

b. _____.

c. _____.

d. _____.

e. _____.

f. _____.

3. What is happening?

a. going to the hospital

b. going in the ambulance

d. arresting the driver

c. calling a garage

a. *The ambulance is going to the hospital.*

b. _____.

c. _____.

d. _____.

149

4. What is going to happen?

a. doctor, operate on the boy

c. judge, hear the case

d. driver, explain
   the accident

e. woman, tell
   her story

b. boy, get well

f. driver, pay a fine

a. *The doctor is going to operate on the boy.*

b. _____.

c. _____.

d. _____.

e. _____.

f. _____.

Subject questions: *Who was driving the car?*

Notice the use of **who** and **what** as subjects:

| **What** | was coming down the street? |
| **A car** | was coming down the street. |

| **Who** | was driving the car? |
| **A man** | was driving the car. |

| **What** | attracted his attention? |
| **A poster** | attracted his attention. |

| **Who** | is arresting him? |
| **A policeman** | is arresting him. |

| **Who** | hears court cases? |
| **Judges** | hear court cases. |

| **Who** | is going to be in court? |
| **The woman and the driver** | are going to be in court. |

Use **who** for persons and **what** for things.

Use the statement pattern for subject questions.

Remember to use the third person singular verb form:

Who **is** going to visit the boy in the hospital?
His mother and father **are** going to visit him.
Who **plays** in the street?
Children **play** in the street.

Practice

Form subject questions about the words in italics, using **who** and **what**. Use a new object, verb, adjective, or adverb according to the picture.

Albert was late for work.
▶ *Who was late for school?*

The letters are on the table.
▶ *What is on the floor?*

Beth and Eve were at the courthouse.
▶

Beth is going to drive the car.
▶

Stanley and Ann are at home tonight.
▶

They are listening to the radio.
▶

The news makes them sad.
▶

Fred and Mary Ann are going to clean the living room.
▶

The shoes were in the box.
▶

The bus was going slowly.
▶

Speak

1. **Victoria:** Didn't you go to the fruit market today?
   Albert: Yes, I did. I went there after work.
   Victoria: Then, where is the fruit?
   Albert: I didn't buy it.
   Victoria: What happened?
   Albert: I forgot the shopping list.

2. **Dolores:** You missed my party, Victoria! What happened to you?
   Victoria: I went to the hospital to see Albert.
   Dolores: Albert? What happened to him?
   Victoria: He and John had a car accident.
   Dolores: Who was driving?
   Victoria: Albert was. He wasn't paying attention, and he didn't see a red light.

Read

Dear Olga,

Christmas is coming soon. The radio stations are playing Christmas music, and the stores are very busy. People are doing their Christmas shopping. Many families have Christmas trees in their homes already. We are going to buy our tree a few days before Christmas.

At this time of the year we make or buy presents for our family. I am going to buy a record for my older brother. He listens to music all the time. I am going to make a toy for my little brother. All of us are going to buy a bracelet for my mother.

Our family is usually together on Christmas Day. My older brother lives in another town, but he always drives his car here. Last year, however, he didn't come because it was snowing very hard and the roads were too dangerous. We all felt very sad.

I hope we are going to be together again this year. My older brother is going to arrive on Christmas Eve. Then we are going to put up the tree in the living room, and we are going to decorate it. We use small electric lights and other decorations. Finally, we put the presents under the tree. We don't open them until Christmas morning.

Do you celebrate Christmas in your country? Write soon.

Your friend,
Elizabeth

155

Answer the questions.
1. When is Christmas coming?
2. Who is playing Christmas music?
3. What are people doing?
4. When is Elizabeth's family going to buy their tree?
5. What is she going to buy for her older brother?
6. What is she going to make for her little brother?
7. Who wasn't home for Christmas last year?
8. What happened last Christmas?
9. What is the family going to do on Christmas Eve?
10. What happens on Christmas morning?

Think

Tonight is Christmas Eve at Elizabeth's house, and all her family is together. Tell about their activities during the Christmas season.

What did they do the week before Christmas?

What are they doing right now, on Christmas Eve?

What are they going to do on Christmas Day?

Pronounce

Contrast [s] and [θ].

sink [s]	think [θ]

snow	discuss	thirsty	birthday
sister	practice	think	Edith
sad	baseball	Thursday	teeth
sell	December	thanks	Kenneth
sold	expensive	three	month

Alice, did you sell your astronomy books?
Yes. Edith sold her books, too.

Was Kenneth sick last month?
Yes, I think he was in the hospital three weeks.

Did the dentist fill some teeth on Thursday?
Yes. He filled three. It was expensive.

Key to Pronunciation Symbols

Vowels and Diphthongs

[iy]	sheep
[i]	ship
[ey]	pain
[e]	net
[æ]	pan, man
[a]	father, socks
[ow]	phone
[ɔ]	Paul, all
[uw]	pool, two
[u]	foot, pull
[ə́]	nut
[ə]	across
[ay]	buy, eye
[aw]	mouth
[ɔy]	boy

Consonants

Voiceless:				Voiced:	
[pʰ]	pan	[p]	nap	[b]	band
[tʰ]	tan	[t]	bat	[d]	day
[kʰ]	can	[k]	back	[g]	good
[f]	fan			[v]	van
[θ]	three, ether			[ð]	they, either
[s]	sip			[z]	zip
[š]	shin			[ž]	leisure
[č]	chin			[ǰ]	jam
				[l]	light
				[r]	right
				[m]	some
				[n]	sun
				[ŋ]	sung

Semiconsonants		Syllabic Consonants	
[y]	yam, yes	[l̩]	apple
[w]	wood	[m̩]	stop 'em
[h]	hood, he	[n̩]	didn't

Stress and Intonation

Syllable stress (within a word): [']
Phrase or sentence stress: [-•-]
Intonation levels:

    4 extra high ——————
    3 high   ——————
    2 mid   ——————
    1 low   ——————

Endings for intonation levels:
    rise   ——————⟋
    sustain   ——————
    fade out ——————⟍

Examples of stress and intonation:

yes/no question: 2 Is he home? (3)

information question: 2 Where is he? (3, 1)

statement: 2 He's sleeping. (3, 1)

with emphasis: 2 He's still sleeping! (4, 1)

Vocabulary List

These are the words introduced in Book 2. The number after each word indicates the page on which it first appears. If a word can be used as more than one part of speech, the way it is used in the text is indicated as follows: n = noun, v = verb, adj = adjective, adv = adverb, prep = preposition, and conj = conjunction.

absent-minded, 122
accident, 141
accountant, 50
acrobat, 109
advertising (n), 57
afraid, 32
Africa, 81
again, 155
agency, 57
ago, 63
agree, 66
agree with, 66
air (n), 123
airport, 57
Alexander, 141
algebra, 81
Allen, 76
almost, 87
alone, 76
already, 155
also, 63
ambulance, 149
animal, 111
Annette, 44
answer (n), 20
apartment, 11
appointment, 107
appropriate (adj), 3
April, 25
arrest (n), 149
arrive, 49

asleep, 123
ate, 95
Atlanta, 48
attention, 151
attract, 151
August, 25
aunt, 126
avenue, 5

Bach, 81
bacon, 59
bacteria, 141
badly, 3
ball, 79
band (n), 59
become, 28
began (past), 95
beginning (n), 3
Ben, 48
Beth, 16
bicycle, 121
birthday, 79
boat (n), 126
Bob, 16
(Laura) Bond, 19
boot (n), 53
bored (adj), 57
boring (adj), 60
Boston (Avenue), 9
bottle (n), 59
bought (past), 96

boulevard, 79
bracelet, 155
brave (adj), 121
breakfast (n), 17
(Susan) Bruno, 51
Burk (Boulevard), 79
business, 48
by accident, 141
by much, 94

cafeteria, 10
cage (n), 113
call (v), 39
came, 109
careful, 43
case (n), 150
Catherine, 60
celebrate, 155
cent, 8
chemist, 57
chocolate, 31
choose, 76
Christmas, 29
Christmas Eve, 155
Christmas tree, 155
circus, 109
classical, 57
Cleveland, 2
cloudy, 45
clown (n), 109
Coleman (Street), 9
(Jane) Coleman, 48
Colorado, 53
concert, 57
contradict, 66
convention, 60
copy (n), 106
court (n), 151
courthouse, 125
cover (n), 108
cut, 33

Dale, 74
dangerous, 155
December, 25
decorate, 155
decoration, 155
definitely, 47
dentist, 32
Denver, 44
department, 1
department store, 1
desk, 93
dessert, 114
Dick, 90
did, 80
die (v), 141
dining room, 137
director, 50
discovery, 141
discuss, 80
discussion, 73
divide (v), 9
dollar, 8
Dolores, 105
Douglas, 44
downtown, 106
dozen, 8
drank, 95
driver, 125
driver's license, 125
drugstore, 11
dull (adj), 108

early, 63
-ed (past), 82
Edmund, 124
education, 81
eighty, 7
electric, 155
elementary school, 11
elephant, 93
end (n), 9

161

enjoy, 57
enough, 47
enter, 123
Ethel, 143
ether, 143
event, 109
everyone, 47
everything, 106
exact (adj), 21
examine, 33
except, 25
excited (adj), 45
exciting (adj), 62
exhibition, 75
explain, 91

face (n), 17
fall (n), 28
fall (v), 29
fall asleep, 123
fan (n), 47
fancy (adj), 47
fantastic, 60
favorite, 57
February, 8
feel, 5
fell (past), 120
felt (past), 122
few, 155
fifty, 7
fill (v), 32
finally, 155
find (v), 57
fine (n), 150
fish (v), 126
fisherman, 126
(Dr. Alexander) Fleming, 141
Florence, 80
Florida, 140

fool (n), 122
foreign, 57
forgot (past), 154
formal (adj), 3
forty, 7
Fred, 104
fresh, 75
fruit, 154
full-time, 56
fun (adj), 74
funny, 108
future, 34

gave, 96
genius, 122
geometry, 81
germ, 141
get, 93
get up, 17
get well, 141
glad, 94
going to, 32
go out, 97
got, 96
grammar, 81
grow, 141

had (past), 95
hair, 33
hairdresser, 33
half, 21
Harold, 24
have time, 44
head (n), 145
hear, 150
heard (past), 123
help (n), 124
Hill (Street), 5
hit (past), 148

hockey, 139
(David) Horgan, 11
hour, 8
Howard, 50
hundred, 7
hurry (n), 76
hurt (past), 144
husband (n), 92
hyphen, 8

ice-skating, 27
individually, 9
in progress, 128
interview (v), 140
introduce, 140
invent, 124
italics, 51

January, 25
jazz, 57
Jean, 10
(Dale) Jensen, 74
Johnson (Street), 9
judge (v), 108
juice, 95
July, 25
June, 25

Kate, 80
Keith, 66
Kennedy (Street), 9
Kenneth, 143
Kent (Street), 93
kill (v), 141
knee (n), 144
knuckle (n), 26

later, 123
Laura, 12
leader, 74
leap year, 25

leaves (n), 29
lecture (n), 33
left (v), 96
license (n), 125
lift (v), 123
light (n), 123
lion, 109
list (n), 154
little, 155
look for, 126
lose, 94
lost (past), 94
lunch (n), 4

magazine, 126
manager, 10
manner, 3
March, 25
(Vincent) Marino, 50
market (n), 154
(Frank) Martin, 50
Mary Ann, 109
May, 25
maybe, 45
(Peter) McCall, 45
meet, 57
meeting, 61
menu, 105
method, 26
midnight, 15
(Ben) Miller, 51
million, 141
Minnesota, 27
miss (v), 154
mold (n), 141
monkey, 108
month, 25
monument, 76
mountain, 45
move (v), 123

much, 91
(Mrs.) Murphy, 16
name (v), 141
Nancy, 32
Nebraska, 30
net (n), 93
(Mr.) Newton, 122
New York (Avenue), 9
next, 33
night club, 78
ninety, 7
noise, 123
north, 28
North America, 28
(Stanley) Novak, 80
November, 8
nut, 108

Oak (Street), 3
ocean, 76
October, 25
of course, 32
official (adj), 21
often, 57
Olga, 155
on business, 48
on the way, 122
on time, 95
one hundred, 7
operate, 33
outside, 122

part-time, 56
past (n), 62
past progressive, 128
Patricia, 13
pay (v), 150
pay attention, 154
penicillin, 141
perfect (adj), 45
Philadelphia, 6

photograph (n), 75
photographer, 126
picnic (n), 28
pitcher, 118
place (n), 3
plan (v), 45
plane (n), 2
plant (n), 28
play (n), 52
player, 56
point (n), 94
police (n), 126
politics, 80
possible, 20
poster, 147
practice (n), 59
prefer, 57
prepare, 137
present (n), 134
program (n), 80
psychiatrist, 33
psychology, 11
put (past), 120
put up, 155

quarter (n), 8

rain (v), 28
rainstorm (n), 128
read (past), 95
really, 75
recent, 109
record (n), 38
red light, 154
refrigerator, 47
regular, 82
relaxed (adj), 76
remember, 26
reply (v), 83
reporter, 140

rest (n), 25
ribbon, 79
ride, 121
ring (n), 113
rink, 139
rock (concert), 74
rode (past), 121
Ronald, 44
(Jane) Ross, 19
rug, 47
rule (n), 83
run (v), 144
Russian, 88
Ruth, 57

salad, 111
salary, 12
Sally, 1
sang (past), 96
Sarah, 3
saw (v), 95
say, 26
schedule (n), 22
season (n), 28
second (n), 8
sell, 1
September, 25
seventy, 7
sharp, 13
shin, 13
shopping (n), 154
sink (n), 157
sixty, 7
ski (v), 45
skiing (n), 29
slept (past), 95
(Mr.) Smith, 10
Smith (Avenue), 5
snow (n), 29
snow (v), 29

sofa, 47
sold, 157
some, 28
something, 12
sometimes, 76
soon, 44
south, 81
South America, 81
spoke (v), 96
spoon (n), 115
spring (n), 28
stamp (n), 126
stand (n), 120
stand up, 123
Stanley, 80
start (v), 82
Steve, 1
St. Louis, 2
stood, 123
storm (n), 128
stove, 47
street, 3
strike (n), 89
subtitle (n), 55
summer, 27
sunny, 45
supper, 123
symphony, 57
system, 124

take, 23
tamer (n), 113
telephone (n), 9
temperature, 45
tent, 93
terrible, 95
test (n), 33
that (conj), 57
therefore, 57
thieves, 123

thirties, 45
thirty, 7
thought (past), 141
ticket (n), 84
tired (adj), 76
told (past), 96
tomorrow, 33
took, 96
tour (n), 76
toy (n), 155
train (n), 26
travel (v), 47
tree, 28
trip (n), 44
trunk, 120
try (v), 83
turn on, 123
two-week, 76

uncle, 125
under, 155
understood, 96
unexpectedly, 125
until, 22
usual, 122
usually, 14

vacation, 29
van, 47
Van Dusen (Street), 13
vase, 120
vegetable, 75
velvet, 79
Victoria, 154
violin, 47

Vivian, 79
vocabulary, 81
volleyball, 53

walk (n), 23
walk (v), 83
Walnut (Street), 3
warm (adj), 28
was, 60
weather (n), 27
weatherman, 45
(Mrs.) Weber, 10
weekend, 42
(Catherine) Wells, 91
went, 96
were, 60
whom, 3
win (v), 94
window, 130
windy, 28
winter (n), 27
(Sandra) Wolf, 50
won, 96
wonderful, 45
world, 141
worry (v), 123
writing (n), 3
wrote, 96

yesterday, 61
yourself, 19

zoo, 108

Index

answers
short, to yes/no questions with
going to, 41
short, to information questions, 53
short, with the past of *be,* 70
short, with *did, didn't,* 102
short, to yes/no questions in past
progressive, 134

be
past of, 62

clock time, 20

days of the week, 52

months, names of, 25

negative
statements with *wasn't, weren't,* 65
short answers with *wasn't, weren't,*
70

numbers
21 to 109, 7

parts of the day, 24

past
of *be,* 62
regular, 82
pronunciation of regular, 82
irregular, 96
progressive, 127

prepositions
in, on, 118

questions
information with *where, what,*
who(m), how, and *do,* 4
information with *when* and *do,* 17
information with *going to,* 50
information with the past of *be,* 73
information in past, 112
information about verb phrase, 115
information with past progressive,
136
yes/no with *going to,* 39
yes/no with the past of *be,* 67
yes/no with *did,* 86
yes/no in past progressive, 132

general with *happen,* 146
subject with *who, what,* 151

sounds
[š] shin, 13
[č] : [š], 31
[f] : [v], 47
[b] band, 59
[b] : [v], 79
[e] net, 93
[ə] nut, 108
[e] : [ə], 124
[θ] ether, 143
[s] : [θ], 157

statements
negative with *wasn't, weren't,* 65
negative in the past with *didn't,* 100

time, expressions of
with *what time,* 20
parts of the day, 24

verbs
past of *be,* 62
regular past, 82
past progressive, 127
negative, 130
yes/no questions in the, 132
short answers to yes/no questions
in the, 134
information questions with the,
136
future with *going to,* 34
negative, 36
yes/no questions with *going to,* 39
short answers to yes/no questions
with *going to,* 41
irregular past, 96

what time
clock time, 20

when
in questions with *do,* 17

who(m), what, where, how
in questions with *do,* 4

who, what
subject questions, 151